CHRISTIAN THEOLOGY
IN AN AFRICAN CONTEXT

Christian Theology
in an African Context

Prof. Timothy Palmer

AFRICA CHRISTIAN TEXTBOOKS

2015

Christian Theology in an African Context

© 2015 by Prof. Timothy Palmer

Africa Christian Textbooks (ACTS)

ACTS Bookshop, International HQ, TCNN,
PMB 2020, Bukuru, Plateau State, 930008, Nigeria
GSM: +234 (0) 803-589-5328; E-mail: info@acts-ng.com
Website: http://www.acts-ng.com

ISBN: 978-978-905-265-3 Print
ISBN: 978-978-905-266-0 ePub
ISBN: 978-978-905-267-7 Mobi

First Printing: 2015

CONTENTS

PREFACE

This is a book about Christian doctrine or theology. It treats the main themes of Christian doctrine starting from the doctrine of God and proceeding to the doctrine of the last things or eschatology.

This book is written in the African context by a non-African who has spent more than 30 years teaching theology in Africa. The particular African context of the author is northern Nigeria; but he has had students from all of Nigeria and beyond. He has also read extensively in African Christian theology.

It is the conviction of this author that the primary source of theology is Scripture (the Bible). But theology is done in a context. In this case, the context is Africa. Theology should be done with an awareness of our African context.

But what is the African context? Is it the traditional world of Chinua Achebe? Or is it the modern urban context of half of the population of Africa? Perhaps it is a mix of the two.

This book is written from an awareness of the traditional and modern African context. But our primary source of theology is Scripture itself. In the end this is a book of Christian doctrine. Who is God? Who is Jesus Christ? What is salvation? What is the church? What does the Bible say about the future?

At the end of the book is an appendix on the history of Christian doctrine. This historical survey will help the student understand the historical context of some of the Christian doctrines. You may want to start with the historical appendix to understand the context of some of our doctrines.

This author is grateful to the African staff and students of the Theological College of Northern Nigeria (TCNN) where he has taught for many years. They have come from a wide diversity of cultural and ecclesiastical backgrounds. This has made doing theology most stimulating and contextual.

It is my prayer that this book will give a theological foundation for the growing church in Africa.

Theological College of Northern Nigeria
Bukuru

CHAPTER 1

DOING CHRISTIAN THEOLOGY

Theology is the reflection on or study of God. Everyone who believes in God does theology. Christians, Muslims and traditionalists do theology.

Often our theology is non-formal; sometimes it is formal. Lay persons and pastors often do non-formal theology. Whenever a person sings or prays or preaches, he or she is doing non-formal theology. African "spirituals" are an example of non-formal theology. Popular publications like church magazines are another type of non-formal theology.[1]

Formal theology, on the other hand, is more academic. This book, for example, is formal theology. Theologians like Augustine of Hippo, Martin Luther, Byang Kato and Kwame Bediako wrote formal theology.

Theology

So what is theology? "Theology" comes from two Greek words: *theos* (God) and *logos* (word). Literally, theology is a word about God. Theology is our human reflection on the nature of God and his activities in the world.

---

[1]See Bulus Galadima, "A Study in Non-Formal African Theology" (Ph.D. thesis, Trinity International University, 1995).

Every religion has a theology. There is Muslim theology, Buddhist theology and Christian theology. This book is a Christian theology.

The question has been asked whether there is one Christian theology or many. In 1976 Ngindu Mushete posited that we have one Christian faith but different expressions of that one faith.[2]

Thus we have denominational theologies such as Methodist, Reformed, Pentecostal and Roman Catholic theologies. Yet despite our denominational differences we hold many things in common like the authority of Scripture, the triune being of God and the atoning work of Christ.

Since the 1960s many have called for regional theologies like African Christian theology. Osadolor Imasogie, for example, argues for an incarnational religion since "theology is never to be done in a cultural vacuum."[3]

But Tersur Aben reminds us of the universality of Christian theology which transcends geographic boundaries. Since Christian theology is "a study of God's nature, words, and deeds," it must be universal.[4]

There is truth in both views. There is both a universality and a particularity to theology. We need to be mindful of our African context but also of the eternal nature of truth.

Theology and Revelation

God is transcendent and distant. So how can we make theological statements about God? How can we know anything about God?

---

[2]See Ngindu Mushete, "Unity of Faith and Pluralism in Theology" in *The Emergent Gospel* (Maryknoll: Orbis, 1978), pp. 50-55.

[3]Osadolor Imasogie, *Guidelines for Christian Theology in Africa* (Achimota: Africa Christian Press, 1983), pp. 20-24.

[4]Tersur Aben, *African Christian Theology* (Bukuru: Africa Christian Textbooks, 2008), p. 50.

The answer lies in God's revelation. God reveals himself to us in different ways. God reveals himself in creation, in Jesus Christ and in Scripture. We do theology on the basis of God's revelation.

Thus revelation is what God does; theology is what we humans do. Theology is our human reflection on God's revelation.

God reveals himself in two basic ways: generally, he reveals himself in creation; specially, he reveals himself in Jesus Christ and in Scripture. There is thus general revelation and special revelation.

There are two types of theology corresponding to these two types of revelation. Natural theology is theology based on God's general revelation; biblical or systematic theology is based on God's special revelation.

Natural theology is our reflection on God's revelation in creation. African traditional religion is an example of natural theology. Our African forefathers (and mothers) who did not know the Bible concluded that God exists. They gave God a name like Chukwu, Aondo or Na'an. They believed that God has attributes like power, justice and love. This is natural theology. This is a theology that responded to God's revelation of himself in creation.

But in time God revealed himself through Jesus Christ and through the Bible. This is special revelation. Biblical or systematic theology does theology in response to God's revelation of himself in the Bible and in Jesus Christ.

Thus God reveals himself, but we theologize. We reflect on God by studying the different revelations of God.

Our African ancestors theologized on the basis of creation but not Scripture; today we can theologize from both creation and Scripture.

Natural theology

So is natural theology good or bad?

The pagan Greek philosophers did natural theology. Plato, for example, used reason and concluded that God exists and that he is the First Cause of the universe; that God is a spirit and that he is perfect; and that God does not suffer.

Our African forefathers (and mothers) also did natural theology. They used reason and concluded that God is all-powerful; that he is the Creator of the world; and that he is just and loving. African traditional religion is a form of natural theology that speaks of God from the African experience of God in creation.

Natural theology is important because it demonstrates that God exists and that God is transcendent. Natural theology is a preparation for the Christian gospel.

But Martin Luther warned us that reason and natural theology can lead us astray.[5] Is it really true that God does not suffer? Natural theology suggests that God does not suffer; but God's revelation of himself in Jesus Christ suggests that perhaps God does suffer.

Further, natural theology is incomplete. Natural theology does not tell us about the Trinity or about the way of salvation. Natural theology does not give a full understanding of the nature of God.

Also, natural theology tends to emphasize the glory of God but not the humility of God. Natural theology does not tell us about the incredible condescension of God in the manger in Bethlehem. Natural theology does not tell us about the suffering of God on the cross.

Natural theology lays a foundation for Christian theology; but biblical or Christian theology will give a greater in-depth understanding of who God is.

---

[5]See M. Luther, "The Last Sermon in Wittenberg," in *Luther's Works* 51:371-80.

Sources of Christian theology

So what are the sources of Christian theology? How do we do Christian theology? Osadolor Imasogie distinguishes subjective and objective sources.[6]

The primary *subjective* source of our theology is the Holy Spirit. Before his crucifixion Jesus promised "the Spirit of truth [who] will guide you into all truth" (Jn 16:13).[7] Imasogie says that "the theologian must remain tuned into the Holy Spirit, the primary source of theology, as he is faced with any human situation."[8] A good theologian will do theology in a prayerful reliance on the Holy Spirit to guide him or her into all truth. The Holy Spirit is our primary subjective source.

The primary *objective* source of theology is Scripture. "As the inspired words of God, the Bible becomes the authentic objective source of the Christian faith. . . . The Holy Bible becomes the primary objective medium by means of which the Living Lord, through the Holy Spirit, continues to disclose God to us."[9]

Tersur Aben agrees. He says that "a viable Christian theology in Africa must derive from the Scriptures." This is the "potent theological principle" of the Reformation, namely, *sola scriptura* (Scripture alone).[10]

Yet Imasogie cautiously allows for other secondary sources. "The secondary objective sources of theology include the Church's dogmatic tradition, human culture and world view, and human historical situations which God uses as occasions for our apprehending his

---

[6]O. Imasogie, *Guidelines for Christian Theology in Africa*, pp. 72-74.

[7]All Scripture references are taken from the New International Version (NIV), occasionally modified to reflect better the meaning of the original Hebrew or Greek text.

[8]O. Imasogie, *Guidelines for Christian Theology*, p. 72.

[9]O. Imasogie, *Guidelines for Christian Theology*, pp. 72-73.

[10]T. Aben, *African Christian Theology*, pp. 181, 183.

self-disclosure." But "these secondary sources must not be over-emphasized."[11]

In a limited sense, our church tradition is a source of theology. A theologian should be aware of the great theologians that went before him or her. These theologians are part of our Christian tradition. But Martin Luther reminds us that in the end Scripture is our final authority. *Sola scriptura*—only Scripture—is the great Reformation principle for doing theology.

In some sense, our culture is a source of theology. A theologian should be aware of one's cultural context. The African culture, for example, has a deep understanding of the spiritual world. This worldview may influence the doing of theology. But culture should not be a primary source of theology. Otherwise we run the danger of syncretism.

Finally, personal experience can be a secondary source of theology. But personal experience can be extremely subjective. Are you sure that it was God who spoke to you in a dream? Personal experience may confirm truths of Scripture but it will not add new information to Scripture.

In the end, the two primary sources of theology are Scripture and the Holy Spirit. Scripture is the primary objective source of theology; the Holy Spirit is the primary subjective source, who enables us to do theology.

---

[11]O. Imasogie, *Guidelines for Christian Theology*, p. 73.

Study Questions

1. What is the difference between revelation and theology?
2. What is natural theology? How can natural theology be useful? What are the limitations of natural theology?
3. What are the primary sources of Christian theology?
4. What are some secondary sources for Christian theology? How useful are these secondary sources?
5. **Essay:** Write an essay on the usefulness of the African culture in the doing of African Christian theology.

CHAPTER 2

REVELATION

God is transcendent and distant. He is hidden. So how can we know God? We know God because he reveals himself to us. As suggested in the last chapter, God reveals himself generally and specially. There is general revelation and special revelation.

General Revelation

General revelation is God's common revelation of himself to every human being. This occurs primarily through creation.

Every person has a partial knowledge of God from creation. We see the sun, moon and stars, and we believe that God created these heavenly bodies. We see the beauty of the flowers and trees, and we confess that a good God made these things. The many remarkable and beautiful animals testify to the wisdom and power of God. Especially the human person is a testimony to the creating power of God.

The book of Psalms says: "The heavens declare the glory of God; the skies proclaim the work of his hands" (Ps 19:1).

Paul writes the Roman church: "Since the creation of the world God's invisible qualities—his eternal power and divine nature—have been clearly seen . . . so that people are without excuse" (Rom 1:20).

In his sermon to the pagans at Lystra, Paul said that God "has not left himself without testimony" for he "has shown kindness by giving you rain from heaven and crops in their seasons" (Acts 14:17).

It is thus surprising that some European theologians deny the fact of general revelation. Karl Barth is one example. Barth believes that God reveals himself decisively in Jesus Christ; therefore all revelation outside of Jesus and Scripture is false.

But the African experience clearly demonstrates the fact of general revelation. Before the coming of the Gospel, most Africans believed in the existence of God. This knowledge of God is a result of God's general revelation in creation.

General revelation is important because it shows that God exists and that he is powerful. General revelation offers a point of contact for those who want to do evangelism. If our people already believe that Chukwu or Oludumare exists, then our task of Christian evangelism has a starting point in this belief in God.

Our knowledge of God from creation is important but it is not a saving knowledge. "The Scriptures make it abundantly clear that all religions without Jesus as the only way end up in unrighteousness and suppression of the truth."[1]

Paul says that even though God's divinity is clearly revealed in creation, sinful humans "suppress the truth by their wickedness" (Rom 1:18). Our sin prevents us from seeing God clearly in creation.

Thus general revelation is not sufficient for salvation. We need a clearer form of revelation.

---

[1]S. Kunhiyop, *African Christian Theology* (Bukuru: Africa Christian Textbooks, 2012), p. 21.

Special Revelation

At significant times in history God revealed himself specifically to certain individuals or people. The author of the book of Hebrews wrote, "In the past God spoke to our ancestors through the prophets at many times and in various ways" (Heb 1:1).

God revealed himself in special ways to Abraham, Isaac and Jacob; he revealed himself to Moses at the burning bush; he spoke to the people of Israel at Mount Sinai; he spoke to all the prophets; and he revealed himself to John on the island of Patmos.

God's revelation of himself in these historical events is called special or particular revelation because these events occurred at particular times in history.

But God's decisive revelation was in the person of Jesus Christ. Although "in the past God spoke to our ancestors . . . in these last days he has spoken to us by his Son, whom he appointed heir of all things, and through whom he made the universe" (Heb 1:1-2).

Jesus is the Word of God, as John proclaims at the beginning of his Gospel: "In the beginning was the Word . . . and the Word became flesh and dwelt among us" (Jn 1:1,14). Since "the Word was with God and the Word was God" (Jn 1:1), Jesus of Nazareth was a unique revelation of God.

Once the apostle Philip wanted to see God the Father. Jesus answered, "Anyone who has seen me has seen the Father" (Jn 14:9). God the Father is hidden; but Jesus is a unique revelation of God. Jesus revealed the deep love and compassion of God. He also revealed God's justice.

The cross of Jesus is perhaps the most profound revelation of the love of God. If Jesus is fully God and if Jesus really suffered on the cross, then the cross deeply reveals the compassion and love of God.

Martin Luther said that natural theology tends to be a theology of glory; but the revelation of God in Christ is a theology of the cross. Natural theology speaks of the power of God; but the theology of the cross speaks of the love and condescension of God.

Luther said that "true theology and recognition of God are in the crucified Christ. . . . God can be found only in suffering and the cross."[2]

Luther is right in telling us that the revelation of God on the cross was a decisive revelation. But it is probably an overstatement to say that God is found *only* on the cross, since God is found also in creation and in Scripture.

But Jesus is no longer with us in the body. So how do we know God now? The Bible is the third main area of God's revelation to us.

The church throughout the centuries has consistently taught that Scripture is the Word of God. Scripture is the clearest revelation of God.

John Calvin once said that creation is like a beautiful book that speaks of God. But our eyes are dim and blurry because of our sin so that we cannot read this beautiful book well. But Scripture is like a pair of spectacles or glasses that allows us to see God clearly again.[3]

The next chapter looks at Scripture as the Word of God.

---

[2]M. Luther, "Heidelberg Disputation," in *Luther's Works* 31:53.

[3]J. Calvin, *Institutes of the Christian Religion* (Philadelphia: Westminster, 1960), p. 70 (1.6.1).

Study Questions

1. How does the African experience testify to the idea of general revelation?
2. Why is general revelation important?
3. Why might general revelation lead to a theology of glory?
4. Evaluate Luther's statement that "God can be found only in suffering and the cross."
5. How is the Bible like spectacles or glasses?
6. **Essay:** Write an essay on natural theology in the African context.

CHAPTER 3

THE BIBLE AS THE WORD OF GOD

When Martin Luther was asked if he would recant his teachings, he said that unless he was convinced "by the testimony of the Scriptures or by clear reason," he would not recant. "My conscience is captive to the Word of God," he said.[1]

The church throughout the centuries has confessed that the Bible is the Word of God. This is a statement of faith based upon evidence in the Bible itself.

Divine and human authorship

Jesus and the apostles considered the Old Testament to be the authoritative Scriptures. Once in a debate with the Jewish leaders, Jesus said that "the Scripture (*graphē*) cannot be broken" (Jn 10:35). The Scripture in this case was the Old Testament.

Paul in 2 Timothy 3:16 said that "all Scripture (*graphē*) is God-breathed (*theopneustos*)." Again, the Scripture here is the Old Testament. The view of Jesus and the apostles is that the canon of the Old Testament Scripture is inspired.

---

[1]M. Luther, "Luther at the Diet of Worms," in *Luther's Works* 32:112.

The *canon* is the inspired books of the Bible. "The canon of Scripture is the list of all the books that belong in the Bible."[2]

The canon at the time of Jesus was the Old Testament. But the early church soon recognized that our New Testament writings are also part of the canon. Therefore both the Old Testament and the New Testament are Scripture (*graphē*). Both the Old and New Testaments are inspired by God.

(Even though the early church defined the canon, it did not create God's Word. Isaac Newton did not create the principle of gravity, but he recognized or defined it. In the same way, the early church did not create the Word of God, but she recognized and defined it.)

A New Testament book was included in the canon if it was apostolic or had a direct link to the apostles. Thus the Gnostic so-called gospels of Mary, Philip, Thomas and Judas were not included in the canon since they were not written by these apostles. These false gospels were written much later.

The second letter to Timothy tells us that all Scripture is *theopneustos* (God-breathed or inspired). Thus all of Scripture has a divine author as well as a human author. This is seen in various places.

The book of Acts tells us that God spoke the words of Psalm 2 by the Holy Spirit through David (Acts 4:25). Peter speaks of the Holy Spirit speaking through David (Acts 1:16). Paul uses similar language about Isaiah's writings (Acts 28:25).

The Gospel of Mark says that David, "speaking by the Holy Spirit," spoke the words of Psalm 110 (Mk 12:36). The Gospel of Matthew tells us that God ("the Lord") spoke the words of Isaiah 7 "through the prophet" (Mt 1:22). The Gospel of Luke says that God spoke through the Old Testament prophets (Lk 1:70).

---

[2]W. Grudem, *Systematic Theology* (Leicester: InterVarsity, 1994), p. 54.

The author of the book of Hebrews says that the Holy Spirit is the author of some Old Testament passages. The Holy Spirit spoke the words of Psalm 95, Jeremiah and Deuteronomy (Heb 3:7; 10:15,17).

Peter at Pentecost tells us that it was God who said the words of Joel (Acts 2:17). Elsewhere the laws of Moses are called "the word of God" (Mk 7:13).

In all the cases above, we notice both the divine author and the human author. God works or speaks through human authors. This is the process of inspiration.

Inspiration

Inspiration literally means "breathing in." This term is related to the Greek *theopneustos* which means "God-breathed" or "inspired by God." The inspiration of the Bible is the work of the Holy Spirit by which he guided the writers of the Bible in what they said. "Scripture is inspired in the sense that God breathed his word to the writers of Scripture."[3]

Paul's words of 2 Timothy 3:16 teach inspiration. In addition, 2 Peter 1:21 describes the process: "For prophecy never had its origin in the will of man, but men spoke from God as they were carried along by the Holy Spirit."

There are various theories of inspiration.[4] The dictation theory says that the Holy Spirit simply dictated the words of the Bible to the authors. But this theory does not give full attention to the human personality of the authors.

The accommodation theory says that "God accommodated himself to the limitations of the human authors."[5] But this theory allows for human errors in the Bible.

---

[3]S. Kunhiyop, *African Christian Theology*, p. 29.
[4]See B. Milne, *Know the Truth* (Leicester: Inter-Varsity Press, 1982), pp. 36-38.
[5]B. Milne, *Know the Truth*, p. 37.

The supervision theory is probably the best theory of inspiration. Here the Holy Spirit supervised and guided the writers of the Bible as they wrote the books of the Bible. The authors were "carried along by the Holy Spirit" (2 Pet 1:21). Yet the distinct personality of each author is seen in the different books.

If Scripture is the Word of God, then it is absolutely reliable in what it intends to teach. The terms *infallibility* and *inerrancy* suggest the utter reliability of the Bible. One author states his understanding of inerrancy: "The Bible, *when correctly interpreted* . . . , is fully truthful in all that it affirms."[6]

At this point exegesis is important. "Exegesis is the process of interpreting the meaning of a text."[7] Proper exegesis is needed to correctly understand the Word of God.

The authority of the Bible

If the Bible, when correctly interpreted, is God's Word, then the Bible is authoritative for our life and our doctrine. John Wesley wrote, "We believe the written word of God to be the only and sufficient rule both of Christian faith and practice."[8]

God's word in creation is ambiguous. Jesus Christ as God's word is no longer physically present with us. But the Bible as God's written word is the clearest revelation that we have of God and of his plan of salvation.

The church has confessed at least two attributes of Scripture. First is the *perspicuity* or clarity of Scripture. Martin Luther wrote: "The Holy

---

[6]M. Erickson, *Christian Theology* (Grand Rapids: Baker, 1983), pp. 233-34. Italics added. Cf. B. Milne, *Know the Truth*, p. 42.

[7]T. Palmer, *Biblical Exegesis Handbook* (Bukuru: Africa Christian Textbooks, 2013), p. 9.

[8]J. Wesley, "The Character of a Methodist," in *Wesley's Works* 8:340.

Spirit is the simplest writer and adviser in heaven and on earth."[9] The Bible is clear enough for the average person to understand its basic teachings.

The second attribute of Scripture is its *sufficiency*. The Anglican *Thirty-Nine* Articles says: "Holy Scripture contains all things necessary to salvation."[10] We do not need any additional source to tell us of the way of salvation. The Bible by itself is a sufficient source.

Byang Kato reminds us of the absolute centrality of Scripture for our theology and life: "in the African evangelical effort to express Christianity in the context of Africa, the Bible must remain the absolute source. The Bible is God's written Word addressed to Africans—and to all peoples—within their cultural background."[11]

Study Questions

1.   How do we know that the Bible is the Word of God?
2.   Define and describe the process of inspiration.
3.   What are the perspicuity and sufficiency of Scripture?
4.   Why is it important to know that the Bible is the Word of God?
5.   If the Bible is the Word of God, why is exegesis important?
6.   **Essay:** Write an exegetical essay on 2 Timothy 3:16-17.

---

[9]M. Luther, "Answer to . . . Emser," in *Luther's Works* 39:178.

[10]"The Thirty-Nine Articles of Religion," in *The Book of Common Prayer* (Abuja, 2007), p. 499.

[11]B. Kato, *Biblical Christianity in Africa* (Achimota: Africa Christian Press, 1985), p. 43.

CHAPTER 4

~~~

THE ATTRIBUTES OF GOD

Both general revelation and special revelation teach us that God exists. But what is God like? What are his attributes? How has God revealed himself?

God's infinity

A person who considers the universe must be amazed by the greatness of God. The number of stars and even galaxies cannot be counted. The Creator of the universe must be infinitely great.

The Bible also testifies to God's majesty and power. The prophet asks, "Who has measured the waters in the hollow of his hand, or with the breadth of his hand marked off the heavens?" God asks, "To whom will you compare me?" (Is 40:12,25).

We can suggest a few attributes relating to God's infinite power.

First, God is *omnipotent* or all-powerful. (The noun is *omnipotence*.) The title "El Shaddai" or "God Almighty" (Gen 17:1) suggests the absolute power of God. The rhetorical question "Is anything too hard for Yahweh?" (Gen 18:14) speaks of God's power. Jeremiah said to God, "Nothing is too hard for you" (Jer 32:17). The psalmist says that God "does whatever pleases him" (Ps 115:3). Jesus said that "with God all things are possible" (Mt 19:26). Both general revelation and special revelation testify to God's power.

Second, God is *omnipresent* or present everywhere. (The noun is *omnipresence*.) The psalmist says, "Where can I go from your Spirit? Where can I flee from your presence? If I go up to the heavens, you are there; if I make my bed in Sheol, you are there" (Ps 139:7-8). God asks, "Am I only a God nearby, and not a God far away? Can anyone hide in secret places so that I cannot see him? Do not I fill heaven and earth?" (Jer 23:23-24). Paul testifies, "The God who made the world and everything in it is the Lord of heaven and earth and does not live in temples built by hands" (Acts 17:24). Jesus said to his disciples, "Surely I will be with you always"—regardless of where they might be (Mt 28:20).

Third, God is *omniscient*, knowing everything. (The noun is *omniscience*.) The psalmist says of God that "his understanding has no limit" (Ps 147:5). The psalmist also says, "You know when I sit and when I rise; you perceive my thoughts from afar" (Ps 139:2). John says, "God is greater than our hearts, and he knows everything" (1 Jn 3:20). Paul testified that "the Spirit searches all things, even the deep things of God" (1 Cor 2:10).

(This doctrine is being challenged today by Open Theism or the Openness Theology which claims that God does not know the future. But the doctrine of the omniscience of God contradicts this theory.[1])

Finally, Scripture tells us that God is *eternal*. He has always existed, and he will always exist. He has no beginning and no end. The psalmist says of God, "Before the mountains were born or you brought forth the earth and the world, from everlasting to everlasting you are God" (Ps 90:2). At the end of the Bible, God said, "I am the Alpha and the Omega ... who is, and who was, and who is to come, the Almighty" (Rev

---

[1]See *The Openness of God* (Downers Grove: InterVarsity, 1994); and J. Frame, *No Other God: A Response to Open Theism* (Phillipsburg, NJ: P&R, 2001).

1:8). Jesus' testimony that "before Abraham was born, I am" (Jn 8:58) suggests the eternity of Jesus' divine nature.

God is infinite in respect to power, space, knowledge and time. For a believer this is comforting.

Attributes of holy love

So how does this infinite God relate to us? One writer summed up God's attributes with the term "holy love."[2] The following attributes express God's holy love.

First of all, God is "holy". In Isaiah's vision, the seraphim proclaimed, "Holy, holy, holy is Yahweh of hosts" (Is 6:3). The four living creatures in Revelation sing a similar song (Rev 4:8). After the exodus from Egypt, the Israelites proclaimed that God is "majestic in holiness" (Ex 15:11). In Leviticus, the people were commanded: "Be holy, because I, Yahweh your God, am holy" (Lev 19:2). Peter repeats this call to holiness for the early church (1 Pet 1:16).

Holiness means that God is set apart in his majesty. In the Old Testament, "the term holiness [was] synonymous with the divine."[3] But holiness also refers to God's ethical purity. The holy God saves those who love him and judges those who disobey him. During the exodus, God was "majestic in holiness," destroying the unbelieving Egyptians and saving the people of Israel. It was also "the Holy One of Israel" who redeemed the Jews from Babylonian captivity (Is 43:3,14,15).

Second, God is *just* or *righteous*. God's justice or righteousness means that he will always do the right thing. The book of Deuteronomy says of God: "his works are perfect, and all his ways are just. A faithful God who does no wrong, upright and just is he" (Deut 32:4).

---

[2]H. Berkhof, *Christian Faith* (Grand Rapids: Eerdmans, 1979), p. 126.
[3]E. Jacob, *Theology of the Old Testament* (New York: Harper, 1958), p. 92.

God is the Judge who always does that which is right. Abraham asks, "Will not the Judge of all the earth do right?" (Gen 18:25). Of course God will do that which is right or just. It is God's nature to always do that which is just or right.

The justice of God suggests that there is a moral or ethical norm in the universe. In the Old Testament, "righteousness is . . . conformity to a norm."[4] A theologian writes: "God's righteousness means that God always acts in accordance with what is right and is himself the final standard of what is right."[5]

At times it may seem that God does not always do that which is just. Job, for example, suggested that God was not always just. But Yahweh appeared to Job in a storm and asked him, "Would you discredit my justice? Would you condemn me to justify yourself? Do you have an arm like God's, and can your voice thunder like his?" (Job 40:8-9). We must recognize that God is God and that we cannot understand him fully. God says, "As the heavens are higher than the earth, so are my ways higher than your ways and my thoughts than your thoughts" (Is 55:9).

God's justice means that he punishes the wicked and rewards the righteous. But who is truly righteous? Paul tells us that "the righteousness of God" is that "the righteous will live by faith" (Rom 1:17). As we will see later, God's plan of salvation through the cross is also just. Believers are righteous because of the just judgment that Jesus received on our behalf.

God's *love* and his justice go hand in hand. The love of God is a central attribute of God frequently mentioned in Scripture. After Moses wanted to see God's glory, God revealed himself by saying, "Yahweh, Yahweh, the compassionate and gracious God, slow to anger,

---

[4]E. Jacob, *Theology of the Old Testament*, p. 94.
[5]W. Grudem, *Systematic Theology*, p. 203.

abounding in love (*chesed*) and faithfulness, maintaining love (*chesed*) to thousands, and forgiving wickedness, rebellion and sin" (Ex 34:6-7).

The Hebrew word *chesed* refers primarily to God's love for his covenant people. Mysteriously, God loved Jacob and hated Esau (Mal 1:2-3). But in a general sense, "God so loved the world" (Jn 3:16). John testifies in his first epistle: "God is love (*agapē*)" (1 Jn 4:16).

The cross of Christ reveals the full extent of God's love. If indeed Christ is God, then the cross reveals the humility and condescension of God. God revealed himself as the "crucified God."[6] It was God himself who was on the cross—out of love for humanity. John writes: "This is how God showed his love among us: He sent his one and only Son into the world that we might live through him" (1 Jn 4:9). "The love of God is the coming and bending down to us of the infinitely high God."[7]

So does God suffer or not? The *impassibility* of God means that he cannot suffer; the *passibility* of God means that he can suffer. The Greek philosophers said that God cannot suffer. Much of Christian theology, influenced by the Greek philosophers, agreed. But Martin Luther said that Jesus reveals "God hidden in suffering."[8] Karl Barth even said that God "essentially and necessarily suffers."[9]

If God suffers, is he then *immutable* or unchanging? In other words, can God change? (*Immutable* means "unchanging.")

Scripture tells us that God cannot change. The prophet Malachi tells us that "I, Yahweh, do not change" (Mal 3:6). James agrees when he speaks of "the Father of the heavenly lights, who does not change like shifting shadows" (Jas 1:17).

---

[6]See J. Moltmann, *The Crucified God* (London: SCM, 1974).

[7]H. Berkhof, *Christian Faith*, p. 130.

[8]M. Luther, "Heidelberg Disputation," *Luther's Works* 31:53.

[9]K. Barth, *Church Dogmatics* IV/1, p. 166.

Perhaps the immutability of God in Scripture means that God is utterly faithful or reliable in his dealings with humanity. His promises never change. One writer speaks of the "unchangeableness of God's faithfulness."[10] Yet the same writer thinks that God changes when he interacts with humanity in salvation history. This happens especially in the incarnation: "In Christ [God] again experienced a profound change when the Word became flesh."[11]

Arguably, God in his essence never changes. But God in his great love interacts with humanity. God feels compassion and sorrow and anger with humanity. God's emotions proceed out of the unchangeableness of his faithfulness. God's emotions and actions proceed out of his holy love.

Study Questions

1.   Define the omnipotence, omnipresence and omniscience of God.
2.   What does Psalm 90 say about the eternity of God?
3.   Explain the holiness of God.
4.   How did the exodus reveal the holiness of God? (See Exodus 15:11).
5.   According to Psalm 7, is God's justice good or bad for a believer?
6.   Is God impassible or passible? Explain.
7.   **Essay:** Compare the attributes of God in African traditional religion with the attributes of God in the Bible.

---

[10]H. Berkhof, *Christian Faith*, p. 147.
[11]H. Berkhof, *Christian Faith*, p. 148.

CHAPTER 5

THE TRINITY

God's identity is defined in part by the Trinity. This doctrine is revealed to us through special revelation.

God is one and three

The Hebrew religion arose in a polytheistic context. The Old Testament rejects polytheism or the belief in many gods. A central confession of the Old Testament was the Shema: "Hear (*shema*), O Israel: Yahweh our God, Yahweh is one" (Dt 6:4). Therefore God says, "You shall have no other gods before me" (Ex 20:3). In Isaiah, God says, "I am Yahweh, and there is no other; apart from me there is no God" (Is 45:5). The Old Testament is strongly monotheistic.

The New Testament is also monotheistic. Jesus reaffirmed the Shema (Mk 12:29). Paul, living in the polytheistic Roman Empire, rejected idols and said that "there is no God but one" (1 Cor 8:4). James affirmed the belief in one God (Jas 2:19).

But Scripture also says that Jesus and the Holy Spirit are divine. John's Gospel opens with the words: "In the beginning was the Word, and the Word was with God, and the Word was God. . . . The Word became flesh and dwelt among us" (Jn 1:1,14). At the end of John's

Gospel, Thomas made his confession of Jesus: "My Lord and my God!" (Jn 20:28).

Paul says that Jesus, "being in very form God," had "equality with God" (Phil 2:6). Elsewhere Paul says that "in Christ all the fullness of the Deity lives in bodily form" (Col 2:9). The author to the Hebrews says that "the Son is the radiance of God's glory and the exact representation of his being" (Heb 1:3).

The Holy Spirit too is divine. Ananias, who lied to the Holy Spirit, "lied not to men but to God" (Acts 5:3-4). The Spirit is the one who "searches all things, even the deep things of God. . . . No one knows the thoughts of God except the Spirit of God" (1 Cor 2:10-11).

The New Testament also contains trinitarian statements that put Father, Son and Holy Spirit as equal. We are to baptize "in the name of the Father and of the Son and of the Holy Spirit" (Mt 28:19). Paul's benediction is also trinitarian: "May the grace of the Lord Jesus Christ, and the love of God, and the fellowship of the Holy Spirit be with you all" (2 Cor 13:14). The Trinity is implied in these statements.

So the trinitarian problem is: how can God be both one and three? How can God be one when the Son and the Spirit are also God?

Historical views of the Trinity[1]

Historically and theologically there are three basic answers to the trinitarian problem. One should choose the best answer.

1. Subordinationism

One solution to the problem is to deny that Jesus and the Holy Spirit are fully God. This is called subordinationism since Jesus and the Spirit are then made subordinate to the Father.

---

[1]See H. Boer, *A Short History of the Early Church* (Ibadan: Daystar, 1976), chapter 9.

Paul of Samosata was the bishop of Antioch from 260 to 272. He said that Jesus was a divinely inspired man but that he was not God. For him there was only one God, namely, God the Father.

In Egypt there was a presbyter called Arius. Arius too held strongly to the oneness of God. But for him Jesus is less than God. Arius said that "there was a time when the Son was not." In other words, for him Jesus is not eternally God.

Nineteenth-century and contemporary liberalism is also subordinationist. Liberal theology thinks that Jesus is a great prophet but not divine. The Mormons and Jehovah Witnesses also deny the full divinity of Jesus.

Subordinationism is an unsatisfactory solution to the question of Trinity since it denies the divinity of Jesus and the Holy Spirit. The Christian church has consistently rejected subordinationism as being unfaithful to the testimony of Scripture.

2. Modalism

Sabellius was a theologian in Rome around 200. Sabellius said that God is one person with three modes of existence. In the Old Testament, God was called the Father; in the Gospels, God is called the Son; after Pentecost, he is called the Holy Spirit.

God is thus *one person* with three different names. Thus Jesus is fully God, but Jesus is not different than the Father or the Holy Spirit. The Holy Spirit would then be divine but not different from the Father or Jesus.

Modalism is attractive because it teaches the oneness of God and also the divinity of the Son and the Holy Spirit. But modalism does not hold to the *simultaneous* existence of Father, Son and Holy Spirit. At the baptism of Jesus, for example, Father, Son and Holy Spirit were all present simultaneously.

The early church rejected modalism as not being faithful to the testimony of Scripture. Tertullian, for example, said that if Sabellius were right, then at the crucifixion the Father would be on the cross and heaven would be empty! This, he said, is impossible.

3. Trinity

The early church rejected the above two solutions and gradually arrived at the doctrine of the Trinity. Athanasius and the Council of Nicea held in 325 rejected the view of Arius. They said that the Word (Logos) is *homo-ousios* or of the same essence as the Father. In other words, the Word is fully divine.

The First Council of Constantinople (381) said that the Holy Spirit is also divine. The early church concluded that Father, Son and Holy Spirit are each fully divine, and yet God is one.

Tertullian, in North Africa, gave Latin terminology to the doctrine of the Trinity. He was the one who invented the word "trinity," which in Latin is *trinitas*. He said that God is one substance in three persons.

But what is a person? The Greek-speaking church spoke of three *hypostaseis* or subsistences. "Person" (persona) is a Latin translation of the Greek. The word "person" is not an ideal word but is simply a human attempt to express the identity of the three.

Trinity today

In contemporary theology there are basically two different directions that one can take in respect to the Trinity. Some theologians stress the oneness of God; others emphasize the threeness.

Karl Barth, for example, did not like the term "person" and instead preferred to talk of "the three 'modes (or ways) of being' in God."[2] His

---

[2]K. Barth, *Church Dogmatics* I/1, p. 355.

concern was to stress the oneness of God, a relevant concern for the north of Nigeria. But his language is very close to the modalism of Sabellius which the early church rejected.

Leonardo Boff on the other hand sees the Trinity as a "perfect community" and thus a model for a socialized community. Father, Son and Holy Spirit are thus three persons who form a perfect community.[3] But is Boff teaching three separate Gods?

As we contextualize this doctrine into the African context, we need to hold onto both the unity and plurality of God. The Muslims remind us of the oneness of God. But Scripture also speaks of threeness. We need to find language that will be faithful to Scripture and relevant to our African context.

In conclusion, a few images may help us to picture this mystery. The sun, its rays and its heat could be an image of the Father, Son and Holy Spirit. Then the Father would be the source; the Son the light; and the Spirit the warmth. And yet there would still be one sun that gives light and warmth.

Again, we can think of a spring of water that produces a stream which creates a lake. The spring would be like the Father; the stream the Son; and the lake the Holy Spirit. Even though they are three things, ultimately they are one body of water.

In the end, though, God as a Trinity is a mystery. All of our language and theology are a feeble attempt to understand God's being.

---

[3]See the title of L. Boff, *Holy Trinity, Perfect Community* (Maryknoll: Orbis, 2000).

Study Questions

1.   What is the trinitarian problem?
2.   What is the Old Testament testimony about the Trinity?
3.   What does the New Testament say about Jesus and the Holy Spirit?
4.   List two trinitarian formulas in the New Testament.
5.   Describe the view of Arius on the Trinity and the response of the Council of Nicea.
6.   Why is Sabellianism attractive? What is the problem with Sabellianism?
7.   **Essay:** Write an essay on your personal understanding of the Trinity in your African context.

CHAPTER 6

CREATION

The universe is amazing. "Our astronomers tell us that there are at least one hundred billion stars in our galaxy alone and easily a trillion such galaxies within the limits of present-day telescopes."[1]

Our earth is a single planet orbiting one of these many stars. The wonderful diversity of life on our earth is striking. The book of Job, for example, talks of mountain goats, wild donkeys, ostriches, horses, hawks, and even the strange behemoth and leviathan (Job 39-41).

So where did our universe come from?

A good creation

Scripture tells us that everything was created by God. The Bible begins with the words, "In the beginning God created the heavens and the earth" (Gen 1:1). Elsewhere we read: "Yahweh is the everlasting God, the Creator of the ends of the earth" (Is 40:28). "God made the earth by his power; he founded the world by his wisdom" (Jer 10:12).

Through Christ the Word "all things were made; without him nothing was made that has been made" (Jn 1:3). In him "all things were created: things in heaven and on earth, visible and invisible" (Col 1:16).

---

[1]E. Achtemeier, *Nature, God, and Pulpit* (Grand Rapids: Eerdmans, 1992), p. 23.

The last book of the Bible confesses that God "created all things, and by [his] will they were created" (Rev 4:11).

The Bible teaches *creatio ex nihilo*—creation out of nothing. Before creation there was only God. At the start of creation there was no pre-existing matter. God created matter out of nothing. This is stated clearly in the book of Hebrews: "what is seen was not made out of what was visible" (Heb 11:3).

Creatio ex nihilo is taught in opposition to the Greek philosopher Plato who said that God used existing matter when he created the world.

Yet creation was a process. The first chapter of Genesis talks of a six-day creation. But we do not know how long a day is in this context. Some claim that a day is a 24-hour period; others assume that the days were long periods of time.

Some scientists posit a Big Bang theory to explain the universe. They say that once, about 13.8 billion years ago, all matter was compressed into a very small place and that this matter exploded and formed our expanding universe: "the chain of events . . . commenced suddenly and sharply at a definite moment in time, in a flash of light and energy."[2] This theory is immensely significant because it states that the universe had a beginning. And if it had a beginning, then there must be a First Cause or a God who started the process.[3]

But other scientists and theologians posit a six 24-hour creation process. These theologians read the Genesis account literally. For such people, the age of the universe would be much younger.

The book of Genesis is not a scientific textbook. The book of Genesis was written to tell us the vital theological truth that the entire

---

[2]R. Jastrow, *God and the Astronomers* (New York: Norton, 1978), p. 14.

[3]R. Jastrow, *God and the Astronomers*, pp. 111-16.

universe came from God. God is the Creator and the Lord of the universe.

So why did God create this vast universe? A classic theologian will say that God created the universe for his glory and honor. But a more practical theologian concludes that "God loves beauty."[4] God loves the vastness of the galaxies and he loves the colors of the birds and butterflies. In the end, God is "worthy . . . to receive glory and honor and power for [he] created all things" (Rev 4:11).

Part of the creation is human beings and spirits who were created with a free will. Why did God create us people? One theologian said, "The act of creation is an act of condescension."[5] God took the risk of interacting with us human beings.

At the end of the creation process God said that it was "very good" (Gen 1:31). Everything that God does and makes is indeed very good.

The Kingdom of God

In a profound sense, the entire universe is the kingdom of God. God is the Creator and the King of the universe. "The biblical idea of kingdom sets our sights on the Creator as the good and wise Ruler of all things, on the loving nature of his reign, and on the realm over which his kingly authority extends. All creatures are God's regal servants."[6]

The Hebrew word *shalom* (peace or well-being) expresses the harmony in God's original creation. "Shalom is the human being dwelling at peace in all his or her relationships: with God, with self,

---

[4]E. Achtemeier, *Nature, God, and Pulpit*, p. 24.

[5]H. Berkhof, *Christian Faith*, p. 157.

[6]G. Spykman, *Reformational Theology* (Grand Rapids: Eerdmans, 1992), p. 265.

with fellows, with nature."[7] God's original creation as the kingdom of God or shalom includes all of created reality.

The doctrine of creation is thus a rejection of the nature-grace dualism. The Greek philosophers thought that nature or matter is bad while spirit is good. So they posited a dualism between physical matter and the spirit.

But the doctrine of creation proclaims that the world of matter and the world of the spirit were originally good. The problem is not physical matter; rather, the problem is sin. Scripture teaches an ethical sin-grace dualism, not a nature-grace dualism.

It is thus wrong to restrict the kingdom of God to "spiritual" or non-physical things. Everything in the world—physical and spiritual—is part of God's kingdom, and is thus important. God is King over all of life.

Some Christians claim that the kingdom of God is found only in the church. But the doctrine of creation reminds us that the kingdom of God extends over all of creation. God is the Creator and King over all of creation.

"Kingdom business" is thus "a total agenda. . . . Our entire life in God's world is called to be kingdom service." We are "servants and citizens in the kingdom of God."[8]

A Christian concept of vocation will recognize that every honorable profession is a calling and is service to the King of creation. Since the entire world is God's creation, every part of life belongs to God. All of life is religious.

This includes our physical environment. It is sad that we have destroyed much of our environment. Forests are chopped down and

---

[7]N. Wolterstorff, *Until Justice and Peace Embrace* (Grand Rapids: Eerdmans, 1983), p. 69.
[8]G. Spykman, *Reformational Theology*, p. 266.

many of our unique African animals are no more to be found. Our environment is polluted with rubbish and plastic bags.

When God created Adam and Eve, he gave a cultural mandate: "Be fruitful and increase in number; fill the earth and subdue it. Rule over the fish of the sea and the birds of the air and over every living creature that moves on the ground" (Gen 1:28). The world was given to us to use and enjoy.

But at the same time, we are stewards of God's creation. The psalmist said, "The earth is Yahweh's, and everything in it" (Ps 24:1). God said to Israel that "the land is mine and you are but aliens and my tenants" (Lev 25:23). God told Adam that he was to "work it" and "take care of" the Garden (Gen 2:15). God is the owner of this world, and we are tenants and stewards of his creation. We should be good stewards of God's creation!

Study Questions

1. What is the Scriptural evidence for creatio ex nihilo?
2. Do you think the universe is old or young? Explain your view.
3. Why do you think God created the universe?
4. Why does Scripture not support a nature-grace dualism?
5. Describe the original kingdom of God.
6. How is the cultural mandate relevant to us?
7. How is the Christian doctrine of creation relevant to our relation to the environment?

CHAPTER 7

THE WORLD OF SPIRITS

The biblical worldview, like the African worldview, presupposes the existence of a world of spirits. But European theologians like Rudolf Bultmann have denied the existence of spirits.[1] In response, Osadolor Imasogie calls the modern European scientific worldview "quasi-scientific," since a truly scientific worldview will acknowledge the existence of both a spiritual and a physical world.[2]

Spirits were a part of God's original creation. The New Testament says that in Christ "all things were created: things in heaven and on earth, visible and invisible, whether thrones or powers or rulers or authorities" (Col 1:16).

Yet the world is now filled with evil spirits. This is supported by the African experience. Byang Kato, for example, said that the traditional "Jaba believe that the whole world is full of spirits. . . . So the life of a Jaba person is dominated by fear."[3] So what does the Bible say about spirits? Where do the evil spirits come from?

---

[1] R. Bultmann said that it is impossible for modern scientific man "to believe in the New Testament world of spirits and miracles" (*Kerygma and Myth* [New York: Harper, 1961], p. 5).

[2] O. Imasogie, *Guidelines for Christian Theology in Africa*, pp. 46-53.

[3] B. Kato, *Theological Pitfalls in Africa* (Nairobi: Evangel, [1975]), p. 36.

Evil spirits

In the beginning, at the end of creation, "God saw all that he had made, and it was very good" (Gen 1:31). This must include the world of spirits.

But two chapters later Satan was tempting Adam and Eve. Therefore, at some point after creation some of the spirits fell. We assume that there was a great rebellion against God and that the rebellious spirits were cast out of heaven. Peter says that "God did not spare angels when they sinned but sent them to hell, putting them into gloomy dungeons" (2 Pet 2:4). Jude likewise talks of "the angels who did not keep their positions of authority but abandoned their own home" (Jude 1:6).[4]

The leader of the rebellion was Satan. Satan is called "the ruler of the kingdom of the air" (Eph 2:2); "the god of this age" (2 Cor 4:4); the "prince of this world" (Jn 12:31; 14:30; 16:11); and "the father of lies" (Jn 8:44). Satan's power is great, but we must remember that Satan is not omnipresent or omnipotent. The power of Satan is always less than the power of God.

Scripture speaks of "the devil and his angels" (Mt 25:41), suggesting that Satan (or the devil) is the leader of the fallen angels.

Under Satan are the demons or the evil spirits. They are many. One demon-possessed man in the Gospels was called Legion, "for we are many" (Mk 5:9). Paul says that our struggle is "against the rulers, the authorities, the powers of this dark world and the spiritual forces of evil in the heavenly realms" (Eph 6:12).

Satan's power is great, but it is less than that of Jesus Christ. When Jesus ascended, he was seated at God's right hand, "far above all rule and authority, power and dominion" (Eph 1:20-21). Therefore we may

---

[4]Isaiah 14 and Ezekiel 28 do not describe the fall of Satan but rather the fall of the kings of Babylon and Tyre. Revelation 12:7-9 describes the defeat of Satan at the cross.

be confident that "neither death nor life, neither angels nor demons, neither the present nor the future, nor any powers . . . will be able to separate us from the love of God that is in Christ Jesus our Lord" (Rom 8:38-39).

Osadolor Imasogie said that a contextual African Christian theology should emphasize "a new appreciation of the efficacy of Christ's power over evil spiritual forces." African Christian theology should teach that Christ is "the all-sufficient conqueror of demons and deliverer from all fears."[5]

Matthew Michael says that "African Christians must be pointed back to the mighty power of Jesus in his ability to protect the believer from the power of witchcraft and evil spirits. . . . [T]he African Christian believer is called to act in the same authority that Jesus exercised during his earthly ministry."[6]

The future of Satan and his demons is clear. The book of Revelation tells us that the devil and his demons will be thrown into the lake of fire (Rev 20:10-15). The end will come after Jesus "has destroyed all dominion, authority and power" (1 Cor 15:24).

Martin Luther in his song "A Mighty Fortress" sang, "The prince of darkness grim, we tremble not for him; his rage we can endure, for lo his doom is sure; one little word shall fell him."

The good spirits

However, we should focus on the good spirits, not the evil spirits. Scripture speaks of a host of heavenly beings who praise God.

The Old Testament pictures God enthroned like an African chief with his court. At the time of Job, the "sons of God" presented themselves before God (Job 1:6; 2:1). At the time of King Ahab, the

[5]O. Imasogie, *Guidelines for African Christian Theology*, pp. 81-82.
[6]M. Michael, *Christian Theology and African Traditions* (Kaduna: Yuty, 2011), p. 164.

prophet Micaiah "saw Yahweh sitting on his throne with all the host of heaven standing around him" (1 Kgs 22:19). The psalmist speaks of God's heavenly host or army that does his will (Ps 103:21).

The heavenly host includes the cherubim who guard the glory of God. Ezekiel's vision gives a graphic portrait of these winged creatures (Ezek 1:10-14; 10:1-22). The same creatures appear in John's vision of God's throne (Rev 4:6-9). Cherubim guard the Garden of Eden (Gen 3:24), and they were on the ark in the tabernacle and in the temple, serving as the throne of God (Ex 25:17-22;1 Kgs 6:23-28; 1 Sam 4:4).

The seraphim are seen only once in the Bible. In his vision Isaiah saw these winged creatures praising God (Is 6:1-6).

Angels appear throughout the Bible. The Hebrew *mal'ak* and the Greek *angelos* mean "messenger." It is assumed that angels are spiritual beings, although they can have a human appearance.[7]

Angels have different functions.[8] In the first place, angels praise God (Ps 103:20; 148:2). At the creation of the world the "sons of God" or the angels rejoiced (Job 38:7). John in one of his visions "heard the voice of many angels, numbering thousands upon thousands, and ten thousand times ten thousand," praising God (Rev 5:11-12; see 7:11). The angels also rejoiced at Jesus' birth (Lk 2:13-15). Praising God is one function of the angels.

A second function of angels is that of messenger. Angels were often sent by God to convey a message or to act on God's behalf. Three men, presumably angels, came to tell Abram that he would have a child (Gen 18:1-15). Two angels rescued Lot and his family from Sodom (Gen 19:1-17).

---

[7]See S. Kunhiyop, *African Christian Theology*, p. 53; M. Erickson, *Christian Theology*, p. 439.

[8]See S. Kunhiyop, *African Christian Theology*, pp. 54-55; M. Erickson, *Christian Theology*, pp. 444-45.

At the time of the birth of Jesus, the angel Gabriel told Zechariah that he would have a child (Lk 1:11-20); the same angel told Mary that she would give birth to Jesus (Lk 1:26-38); and an angel of the Lord announced the birth of Jesus to the shepherds (Lk 2:9-12). An angel also came to Joseph three times with a message (Mt 1:20; 2:13,19).

Angels also minister to believers. Angels will guard and protect believers (Ps 34:7; 91:11-12). Angels are "ministering spirits sent to serve those who will inherit salvation" (Heb 1:14). The angels rejoice when a sinner repents (Lk 15:10).

A truly scientific worldview will recognize the existence of the spirit world. Prof Imasogie says: "any theology that does not interact with this perception of reality will be irrelevant to those Africans who hold such a world view."[9]

Ancestral spirits

Every human person has a spirit. So what happens to the spirit of our ancestors when they die?

The Old Testament had an undeveloped eschatology. In the Old Testament, Sheol was the place where the ancestral spirits went. Isaiah gives a vivid picture of Sheol at the death of the king of Babylon: "Sheol below is all astir to meet you at your coming; it rouses the spirits of the departed to greet you—all those who were leaders in the world . . . How have you fallen from heaven, O morning star, son of the dawn!" (Is 14:9-12).

In the New Testament, Hades is often the equivalent of Sheol. Sometimes Hades is the place of the dead (see Acts 2:27,31); at other times, Hades is a designation for hell (see Mt 16:18; Lk 16:23).

The New Testament eschatology is more defined than that of the Old Testament. The spirits of unbelievers will go to hell, while the

---

[9]O. Imasogie, *Guidelines for Christian Theology in Africa*, p. 77.

spirits of believers will go to heaven. The parable of the rich man and Lazarus says that the rich man went to torment in Hades, while Lazarus was at Abraham's side (Lk 16:22-24).

The spirits of believers who die will be with Jesus. Jesus told the thief on the cross that "today you will be with me in paradise" (Lk 23:43). Paul had the desire "to depart and be with Christ" (Phil 1:23). He preferred to be away from the body and at home with the Lord (2 Cor 5:6).

Scripture tells us that the spirits of our ancestors are alive. But they are not with us on this earth. Instead they are in heaven or in hell.

Study Questions

1.   Why is a worldview that denies spirits "quasi-scientific"?
2.   Where do Satan and the evil spirits come from?
3.   Who is the fallen morning star in Isaiah 14:12? Consider the context of this verse in your explanation.
4.   Describe the heavenly host in Job and in 1 Kings 22.
5.   What are the functions of the angels?
6.   **Essay:** Write an essay on a Christian perspective on the ancestral spirits.

CHAPTER 8

THE HUMAN PERSON

"What is man?" the psalmist asks (Ps 8:4). This is an extremely relevant question. Who are we really?

In our time, many answers have been given. We will consider a few of them.[1]

- *Liberalism,* especially before World War I in Europe, taught the essential goodness of humans.
- *Existentialism,* after the brutal World War I in Europe, concluded that we humans are either demons or lost persons in the universe.
- *Freudianism,* pioneered by Sigmund Freud, concluded that a person is a sexual being.
- *Marxism,* named after Karl Marx, assumed that we are units in an economic system. Economic reality is then everything.
- *Materialism* assumes that a human person is made up of only physical-chemical elements, and therefore is without a soul or spirit.
- *The technological society* sometimes assumes that humans are only productive machines in our economy.

---

[1]See M. Erickson, *Christian Theology,* pp. 462-70; G. Spykman, *Reformational Theology,* pp. 207-15; J. R. Williams, *Renewal Theology* (Grand Rapids: Zondervan, 1996), 1:197-98.

- *Evolutionism,* following Charles Darwin, assumes that the human being is simply the most successful animal in the supposed evolutionary process.

The traditional African worldview emphasizes our value as part of our community. Ifeanyi Menkiti said that "in the African view it is the community which defines the person as person."[2] As John Mbiti said, "I am because we are, and we are because I am."[3]

So what does the Bible say about our identity?

The image of God

The first creation story tells us that *adam* was made in the image and likeness of God (Gen 1:26-27). In other words, we are like God. So how are we like God? We are like God in two ways: in structure and in function.[4]

Structurally, we are like God because we can reason and will in a different way than the animals. Humans are capable of abstract thought and deep emotions unlike those of animals. Believers and unbelievers have mental and emotional qualities like God.

Functionally, we are like God in our original holiness and righteousness. Paul says that the renewed person is like God in "true righteousness and holiness" (Eph 4:24) and in renewed knowledge (Col 3:10). This suggests that man and woman before the fall were originally holy, just and righteous.

The Genesis creation accounts suggest that human beings were created in a threefold relationship. We were created in a good

---

[2]I. Menkiti in *African Philosophy* (Langham, Md.: University Press of America, 1984), p. 172; quoted by M. Michael, *Christian Theology and African Traditions*, p. 168.

[3]J. Mbiti, *African Religions and Philosophy* (New York: Doubleday, 1970), p. 141; quoted by M. Michael, *Christian Theology and African Traditions*, p. 176.

[4]A. Hoekema, *Created in God's Image* (Grand Rapids: Eerdmans, 1986), pp. 68-73.

relationship with God, our fellow human person and nature. Originally Adam and Eve lived in harmony with God, with each other and with creation.[5]

Sin corrupted but did not destroy the image of God in us. After the fall there are still references to the image of God in the fallen person. For example, after the flood, God said that it is wrong to murder another human being "for in the image of God has God made man" (Gen 9:6). James in his epistle tells us that all people are still in God's likeness (Jas 3:9).

Redemption in Christ restores the fallen image. The new person "is being renewed in knowledge in the image of its Creator" (Col 3:10). The new person is "created to be like God in true righteousness and holiness" (Eph 4:24).[6]

It is clear from the image of God that a human person is essentially a religious person. We are created in a good relationship with God; sin corrupted this relationship; salvation in Jesus Christ restores this relationship. *Creation-fall-redemption is the key for understanding the human person.*

Body, soul and spirit

So how is a human person constituted? How many parts does a person have?

Scripture uses different terms to describe the human person: body, flesh, soul, spirit, heart, mind and strength. On the basis of this, three main positions have emerged.[7]

---

[5]A. Hoekema, *Created in God's Image*, pp. 75-82.
[6]A. Hoekema, *Created in God's Image*, pp. 83-91.
[7]See M. Erickson, *Christian Theology*, pp. 520-539; W. Grudem, *Systematic Theology*, pp. 472-82; A. Hoekema, *Created in God's Image*, pp. 203-226.

Trichotomy is the belief that a person has three parts: body, soul and spirit. The two main texts to support this view are 1 Thessalonians 5:23 ("May your whole spirit, soul and body be kept blameless") and Hebrews 4:12 ("The word of God . . . penetrates even to dividing soul and spirit"). But what is the difference between the soul and the spirit? Perhaps they are two synonymous words for the non-physical part of a person.

Dichotomy believes that a human person has two parts: the physical body and the non-physical spirit or soul. Dichotomy assumes that soul and spirit are two synonymous terms for the non-physical part of a person.

Monism believes that a human person will always be with a body, even after death. Monism says that it is not possible to separate body and soul. Thus, when a believer dies, he or she is immediately with Christ in his or her resurrected body.

A few observations can be made.

First, Scripture often uses a variety of overlapping terms for the human person. An Old Testament scholar calls this the "stereometric" (or overlapping) use of terms.[8] For example, you are to love God "with all your heart and with all your soul and with all your strength" (Deut 6:5). But Jesus said, "Love the Lord your God with all your heart and with all your soul and with all your mind and with all your strength" (Mk 12:30). Does a person now have four parts, or are these terms used stereometrically?

Second, often in Scripture soul and spirit are often used synonymously for the non-physical part of a person. A person is described as having a body and soul in Matthew (10:28) but a body

---

[8]H.H. Wolff, *Anthropology of the Old Testament* (London: SCM, 1974), pp. 7-9; quoted by T. Palmer, "A Theology of the Old Testament" (Bukuru: Africa Christian Textbooks, 2011), p. 37.

and spirit in 1 Corinthians (7:34). Mary, using Hebrew parallelism, says that her soul praises God and her spirit rejoices in God (Lk 1:46-47), implying that they are the same. In one place in John's Gospel, Jesus' soul was troubled (Jn 12:27), and elsewhere his spirit was troubled (Jn 13:21). The believing dead can be called "spirits" (Heb 12:23) or "souls" (Rev 6:9).

Finally, what happens during the intermediate state (the period between one's death and the final resurrection)? Jesus said to the thief on the cross, "Today you will be with me in paradise" (Lk 23:43), suggesting that the spirit and/or soul would go to heaven while the body would go to the grave. Paul suggests the possibility of being "away from the body and at home with the Lord" (2 Cor 5:8). We assume that when we die, the body will go to the grave and the spirit/soul of the believer will be in heaven.

The heart

A final term should be brought into the picture. The heart is a basic biblical word, often referring to the religious center of a person. (Usually the word "heart" refers to the non-physical part of a person, not the physical heart.)

"The heart represents the unifying center of a person's entire existence. . . . The heart is . . . the focal point of religion, that is, of life."[9]

The heart is "the wellspring of life" (Prov 4:23). From the heart "come evil thoughts, sexual immorality, theft, murder" and the like (Mk 7:21-22). But other people are "pure in heart" (Mt 5:8).

Moses commanded Israel to love God with all their heart, soul and strength (Deut 6:5). But Jeremiah said that "the heart is deceitful above all things" (Jer 17:9). Yet God promised Israel a renewed heart: "I will give you a new heart and put a new spirit in you" (Ezek 36:26).

---

[9]G. Spykman, *Reformational Theology*, p. 218.

"The heart is . . . the focal point of religion, that is, of life. For life is religion."[10] The heart is the religious center of a person which governs all of his or her life activities. The heart is thus essentially synonymous with the soul or spirit.

Study Questions

1.   Describe the shortcomings of evolutionism, Marxism and materialism in respect to anthropology.
2.   What is the image of God in a person?
3.   Describe the renewed image of God in a Christian.
4.   Why might the intermediate state be a problem for the monist view of a person?
5.   When is the soul created?
6.   **Essay:** Write an essay defending the trichotomist, dichotomist or monist view of the person.

---

[10]G. Spykman, *Reformational Theology*, p. 218.

CHAPTER 9

EVIL AND SIN

The creation account proclaims that in the beginning everything that God made was "very good" (Gen 1:31). Yet in our world there is an enormous problem of evil.

Evil is something that is not good. There are two types of evil: moral evil, or sin; and natural evil, or disasters.[1] So where do moral evil and natural evil come from?

The origin of evil

Moral evil is sin. So if God is good and his original creation was very good, where did moral evil come from? There are a few possible explanations.[2]

A *monist* solution will say that everything has a single cause, namely, God. (*Monism* is related to the Greek word for "only.") Thus monism says that God is the source of sin. God is then to be blamed for the fact of sin. But this has a major theological problem since God is

---

[1]The Old Testament uses the Hebrew word *ra* for both moral evil and natural evil. The KJV consistently uses "evil" for both; contemporary translations like the NIV use "evil" for moral evil and "disaster" for natural evil. See T. Palmer, *A Theology of the Old Testament*, chapter 6

[2]See G. Spykman, *Reformational Theology*, pp. 306-12.

holy and is always against evil. How can a holy God be the origin of sin? One theologian says: "Evil has no divine origin, not even 'in a certain sense.' . . . The power of evil is 'the greatest contradiction tolerated by God in his creation.'"[3]

A *dualist* solution thinks that evil has always existed outside of God. Manicheism is an old religion in ancient Persia which said that from eternity there were two gods: a good God and an evil god. For them the evil god is the origin of moral evil. Manicheism influenced Marcion, who also said that there are two gods. But the church has consistently rejected such dualism. In the beginning there was God—and nothing else.

A *demonic* solution says that evil comes from Satan and his demons. This is a popular solution. If you sin, it is easy to say, "The devil made me do it!" But the theological and philosophical question is: "Where did an evil Satan come from?" The demonic solution is not a final solution to the problem of the origin of moral evil.

All three solutions above are inadequate. The origin of evil in God's good creation remains a mystery. One theologian says: "The *origin* of evil remains an inexplicable mystery. But its *beginning* is a matter of biblical record."[4]

The biblical record tells us that in the original Garden of Eden there was no evil. (There was a tree of the knowledge of good and evil, but the knowledge of evil and the actual existence of evil are not the same.) There was no evil in the original garden.

The biblical record in Genesis tells us that Adam and Eve were created good, but at some point in time they decided to do evil. In other words, Adam and Eve had free will, which means that their will was free

---

[3]G. Spykman, *Reformational Theology*, p. 307.
[4]G. Spykman, *Reformational Theology*, pp. 311-12.

to choose good or evil. At first, their will chose the good path of service to God; later, they willed to rebel against God and to follow Satan.

The same thing happened earlier to Satan and his angels. They too had the free will to choose to serve God or to rebel against him. But at some point in time, some of the angels chose to rebel against God while others chose to serve God. This is the use—or misuse—of free will.

Did God know that humans and angels would fall? If God foreknew the fall, why did he allow it? We don't know the answers to such questions. God said to Job, "Who is this that darkens my counsel with words without knowledge?" (Job 38:2). We don't know the mind of God, but we do know that we are guilty. We are the ones who have sinned.

Natural evil is a consequence of moral evil. This is clear from Genesis. There we read that death and suffering are a consequence of sin. Human death came as a result of Adam and Eve's disobedience to God. Pain in child-birth and thorns on the farm are also a result of the first sin.

Original sin

The first sin of Adam and Eve is sometimes called the original sin since it was the first sin of us humans. This original sin was a sin of disobedience to God. In a sense, it was the sin of pride since Adam and Eve wanted to be "like God" (Gen 3:5).

The term "original sin" refers first of all to the first sin of Adam and Eve. But "original sin" also refers to the sin that we have inherited from Adam and Eve.

Paul says in Romans that "sin entered the world through one man [Adam], and death through sin, and in this way death came to all persons because all sinned .... Through the disobedience of the one man [Adam] the many were made sinners" (Rom 5:12,19).

Original sin is the sin that we inherited from Adam (and Eve). Through Adam, our corporate head, we are all corrupt and guilty. Through Adam our human nature is now corrupt. Through Adam we are born with a sinful nature. Through Adam we now deserve God's punishment.

But, you may say, this is not fair! Why should we be punished for Adam's sin?

This question is an individualistic question. In Africa we have a greater appreciation of community. What an individual does affects the rest of his or her community.

Furthermore, we have all sinned and deserve punishment on the basis of our own sins. We are guilty not just because of Adam's sin but also because of our own sins.

The essence of sin

So what is the essence of sin?

First, the Genesis story suggests that the primary sin is that of pride or rebellion against God. Adam and Eve wanted to be like God. They wanted to put themselves in the place of God, or at least be on the same level as God.

St. Augustine said that the first human sin and the basic sin is the sin of pride. Pride is putting one's self in the place of God. Pride is assuming that we are greater than God.

Pride is a form of rebellion against God. Isaiah tells Israel that their sin was that they rebelled against God (Is 1:2). In Jeremiah, God accuses Israel: "You have all rebelled against me" (Jer 2:29).

Paul says that the sinful mind "is hostile to God. It does not submit to God's law, nor can it do so" (Rom 8:7).

In the second place, sin is breaking God's law. John writes: "Everyone who sins breaks the law; in fact, sin is lawlessness [*anomia*]" (1 Jn 3:4).

God's law was revealed on Mount Sinai to the people of Israel. But even traditionalists or Gentiles "who do not have the law . . . are a law for themselves . . . since they show that the requirements of the law are written on their hearts" (Rom 2:14-15). Scripture presupposes that every human person knows the law of God. Every human person knows what is right and what is wrong. Our conscience and our culture tell us generally what is right and what is wrong.

Thirdly, sin is destroying the *shalom* or well-being of God's original creation. "God hates sin not just because it violates his law but, more substantively, because it violates shalom, because it breaks the peace, because it interferes with the way things are supposed to be. . . . In short, sin is culpable shalom-breaking."[5]

Sin is thus an offence not only against God but also against our fellow human being. Corruption, adultery, cheating, tribalism and envy are offences not only against God but also against our neighbor.

In short, sin is "not the way it's supposed to be."[6]

The guilt of sin

Many African cultures have the myth of the woman who while pounding yams hit God in his face and caused him to retreat. The Bible agrees with the theology of this myth. Our sins have offended God and caused him to retreat.

Paul tells the Colossians: "Once you were alienated from God and were enemies in your minds because of your evil behavior" (Col 1:21). Paul tells the Romans that once "we were God's enemies" (Rom 5:10).

---

[5]C. Plantinga, *Not the Way It's Supposed To Be* (Grand Rapids: Eerdmans, 1995), p. 14.
[6]See the title of C. Plantinga's book: *Not the Way It's Supposed To Be: A Breviary of Sin.*

Our sins made us guilty before God and subject to God's wrath. Paul writes: "the wrath of God is being revealed from heaven against all human godlessness and wickedness" (Rom 1:18). Paul continues: "you are storing up wrath against yourself for the day of God's wrath, when his righteous judgment will be revealed" (Rom 2:5).

But God's wrath is not an arbitrary emotion. "Rather, God's wrath is altogether determined by his righteousness and holiness."[7] There is a universal standard of justice and righteousness which demands righteousness of every person.

This standard of justice is found in God's law, especially the law revealed to Israel at Mount Sinai. The law says that those who are righteous shall be rewarded, and those who are sinful will be punished. Paul explains this to the Galatians by quoting Deuteronomy: "Cursed is everyone who does not continue to do everything written in the Book of the Law" (Gal 3:10; cf. Deut 27:26).

Our human situation is not good. We are polluted and corrupted with sin; and we are guilty, deserving punishment.

There has to be a solution.

---

[7]H. Ridderbos, *Paul* (Grand Rapids: Eerdmans, 1975), p. 109.

Study Questions

1. Explain and evaluate the monist and dualist solutions to the problem of evil.
2. Does the existence of the tree of the knowledge of good and evil in the Garden of Eden imply that there was already evil in the Garden? Explain.
3. What is the origin of moral evil?
4. What is original sin?
5. What is the essence of sin?
6. Describe and distinguish our corruption and our guilt.

CHAPTER 10

THE RULE OF GOD IN HISTORY

The world is God's kingdom. God is the king over his kingdom. But things have gone wrong in the world. Evil forces have taken over. Part of the world is now Satan's kingdom.

Evil has entered God's kingdom because of the freedom that God gave to the spirits and us people. So what is the solution to the problem of evil?

God's plan

It is clear from Scripture that God has a plan or a purpose. His purpose is redemptive or salvific. His purpose is the redemption of the world.

God's plan is hinted at in the beginning of Genesis. After Adam and Eve ate of the fruit, God told the serpent—who was Satan—that the seed or offspring of Eve would crush the head of the serpent (Gen 3:15).

God's plan is suggested in the call of Abram. At that time God said that all peoples on earth would be blessed through Abram (Gen 12:3).

God's plan is alluded to after the exodus at Mount Sinai. Then Israel was called "a kingdom of priests and a holy nation" (Ex 19:6). God had a plan for Israel to be models of holiness in his world.

God's plan is spoken of to the exiles in Babylon. Then God spoke of "the plans I have for you . . . plans to prosper you and not to harm you" (Jer 29:11).

The New Testament also speaks of God's plans and purpose. Believers have been called according to God's purpose (Rom 8:28). Believers are also chosen "according to the plan of him who works out everything in conformity with the purpose of his will" (Eph 1:11).

Significantly, the death of Jesus was a central part of that plan. Jesus was handed over "by God's set purpose and foreknowledge" (Acts 2:23).

God has a plan of salvation for the world. God's purpose is redemptive. There is a plan of salvation for the world and the cosmos.

God's activity in human history

It is also clear from Scripture that God acts in history in order to fulfill his plan. (The activity of God in history is sometimes called the doctrine of providence.) God acts in history in different ways.[1]

First, God controls the world of nature. God "makes clouds rise from the ends of the earth; he sends lightening with rain and brings out the wind from his storehouses" (Ps 135:7). God cares for the animals. "These all look to [God] to give them their food at the proper time" (Ps 104:27).

In the story of Jonah, God sent a great wind, a great fish, a vine, and a worm to destroy the vine (Jon 1:4,17; 4:6-7). The book of Amos tells us that God caused famine, drought, pestilence and plagues (Amos 4:6-10). At the time of Elijah, God caused a long drought and then a heavy rain (1 Kgs 17:1; 18:45).

Second, God acts in the history of nations. God "changes times and seasons; he sets up kings and deposes them" (Dan 2:21). God used the Assyrian armies to destroy Samaria and take Israel into captivity (2 Kgs

---

[1]See M. Erickson, *Christian Theology*, pp. 394-98.

The Rule of God in History   63

17:7,18; Is 10:5-7). Babylon was God's "war club" to "shatter nations" and "destroy kingdoms" (Jer 51:20).

Jesus was put to death "by God's set purpose and foreknowledge" (Acts 2:23). When King Herod, Governor Pilate and the Jewish leaders crucified Jesus, they did that which God's "power and will had decided beforehand [would] happen" (Acts 4:27-28).

Third, God acts in the lives of individual persons. Job in his suffering said: "Yahweh gave and Yahweh has taken away; blessed be the name of Yahweh" (Job 1:21). After receiving a son, Hannah said: "Yahweh brings death and makes alive; he brings down to Sheol and raises up. Yahweh sends poverty and wealth; he humbles and he exalts" (1 Sam 2:6-7). When Mary was told that she was with child, she said, "[God] has brought down rulers from their thrones but has lifted up the humble" (Lk 1:52).

God also caused Joseph's brothers to sell him into slavery into Egypt. When the brothers came to Egypt, Joseph told them that it was God who sent him to Egypt: "It was not you who sent me here, but God" (Gen 45:8).

The Joseph story shows us that in history there is often a divine agent (or actor) and a human agent (or actor) in the same event. Who sold Joseph into slavery? Both God and Joseph's brothers acted. Joseph said to his brothers, "You intended to harm me, but God intended it for good" (Gen 50:20).

When Assyria destroyed Samaria, there were two agents or causes: God and the Assyrian king. God "sent him" against Israel for a holy purpose; but the Assyrian "purpose was to destroy" (Is 10:6-7). One event had two agents or causes with two separate purposes.

Likewise, when Jesus was crucified, Herod, Pilate and the Jewish leaders had an evil purpose; but God had a redemptive purpose (see Acts 4:27-28).

So does God cause everything that happens in history? How does God act in history?

Models of providence

Providence is the belief in God's activity in history. A few models of providence can be mentioned.[2] A person should choose the best model.

Deism is an 18th-century European idea that God created the world with natural laws. After this creation God withdrew and allowed the world to run on its own according to its natural laws. In that case, the world is like a watch that a watch-maker wound up and allowed to run by itself. But this view is contradicted by Scripture which says that God is continually active in human history.

John Calvin's doctrine of providence teaches that every act in human history has both a divine and human cause. For him God's will is the primary cause of every act, and our human will is the secondary cause. Thus God is the final cause of everything in the world, both good and bad. Calvin believed that despite the evil in the world God is taking care of believers and leading the church to a good end. This view should be a comfort to believers in times of trouble.[3] This is the Calvinistic model.

But some theologians say that this view does not do justice to our human freedom or choices. The Redemptive-Intervention model gives the human person greater freedom. In this view God knows the future but he does not cause everything that happens. Yet God has an overall goal or plan for the world. God at times intervenes in history to respond to the prayers of believers and to direct history to its end.

---

[2]See T. Tiessen, *Providence and Prayer* (Downers Grove: InterVarsity Press, 2000); W. Grudem, *Systematic Theology*, pp. 315-51.
[3]J. Calvin, *Institutes of the Christian Religion*, Book 1, chapters 16-18.

The Open Theism model says that God does not know the future but he may respond to events in history.[4] This view is a solution to the problem of evil. But this view is contradicted by the doctrines of the omnipotence and omniscience of God.

A Christian should prayerfully consider these big questions. Does God cause everything that happens? Does God cause or allow evil to happen? Does God know the future?

One theologian calls attention to the "paradox of God's direction and government on the one hand and the free activity of His creatures on the other."[5] There is a paradox between God's sovereignty and our human freedom.

The problem of evil is an important factor in this discussion. Does God cause evil?

We know that God may cause natural evil or disasters. In reference to the Babylonian captivity, God said: "I form the light and create darkness, I bring prosperity (*shalom*) and create disaster (*ra*)" (Is 45:7). The "evil" (*ra*) in this case may have been the Babylonian captivity. We have also seen above that God also caused the natural evils of famine and drought and the like (Amos 4:6-10).

But there is a reluctance on the part of theologians to say that God causes sin or moral evil. This reluctance became more acute after the German execution of 6 million Jews in concentration camps like Auschwitz during the Second World War.

Once in a German concentration camp, a child was being hanged on the gallows. One of the people watching this horrible event asked, "Where is God now?" And then a Jewish man thought, "Where is He?

---

[4]See *The Openness of God*, ed. C. Pinnock et al.
[5]J. Williams, *Renewal Theology*, 1:125.

Here He is—He is hanging here on this gallows."[6] Maybe God is next to those who are suffering.

Scripture also teaches us that God works in history for his people. Paul says that "in all things God works for the good of those who love him, who have been called according to his purpose" (Rom 8:28).

The doctrine of providence teaches us that God has a redemptive plan for the world. God is active in history. But theologians differ as to how God acts in history.

Study Questions

1. Describe God's redemptive plan.
2. Describe and evaluate John Calvin's doctrine of providence.
3. Does God cause moral and natural evil? Explain.
4. Who sold Joseph into slavery according to Genesis 45:4-8?
5. You are a pastor at a graveside. How would Job 1:21 be relevant to what you might say?
6. Where was God when the Boko Haram attacked Borno State?
7. **Essay:** Write an essay on your personal understanding of providence or God's activity in history.

---

[6]Elie Wiesel, *Night* (New York: Avon Books, 1960), p. 76.

CHAPTER 11

COVENANT AND LAW

God's redemptive plan—after the opening chapters of Genesis—began with Abraham. Most of the Old Testament deals with God's interaction with Abraham's family and Israel. In this redemptive history God often works through covenants.

Covenant

The covenant is God's preferred way of dealing with his people. God made various covenants throughout redemptive history.

A covenant is "a solemn promise made binding by an oath."[1] There are both unconditional (unilateral) and conditional (bilateral) covenants.[2]

Unilateral covenants are unconditional acts of grace from God. The covenant with Noah is God's promise not to destroy the world again with a flood (Gen 9:8-17). The first covenant with Abraham is God's promise of children and land (Gen 15). The covenant with David is a promise of an eternal throne (2 Sam 7:14-16; Ps 89). In each case God shows his love or favor to us.

---

[1]G. Mendenhall, "Covenant" in *Interpreter's Dictionary of the Bible* (Nashville: Abingdon, 1962), 1:714-15.

[2]See T. Palmer, *A Theology of the Old Testament*, chapter 9.

But conditional or bilateral covenants establish a relationship between God and his people. God first established a bilateral covenant with Abraham. We find this in Genesis 17. There God promised to be Abraham's God, and Abraham and his family promised to be faithful to God. This covenant was sealed by male circumcision.

Later at Mount Sinai God entered into a mutual covenant with Israel. We find this in Exodus 19-24. There God entered into a redemptive relationship with Israel. Jeremiah says that Israel became God's bride at Mount Sinai (Jer 2:2).

The summary of the covenant is: "I will . . . be your God, and you will be my people" (Lev 26:12). The covenant creates a relationship of love and salvation between God and his people. It is like a marriage relationship.

The Sinaitic covenant ceased at the end of the Old Testament. Then God made a new covenant. Jeremiah prophesied this new covenant: "The time is coming when I will make a new covenant . . . . I will be their God, and they will be my people" (Jer 31:31-33). Again, a relationship of love is established between God and his people.

The book of Hebrews tells us that the new covenant was fulfilled in Jesus Christ. Jesus is the "mediator" of this new covenant (Heb 8:6). From the Last Supper we learn that the blood of Jesus shed on the cross is the "blood of the covenant, which is poured out for many." The eucharist cup is a memory of Christ's blood of the covenant (Mk 14:24).

The New Testament again uses the metaphor of marriage to express the covenant relationship. The relationship between Christ and the church is compared to the relationship of love between a husband and a wife (Eph 5:22-33). The church is Christ's bride (Rev 21:2).

The new covenant is a redemptive covenant. Those who believe in Jesus will be saved. The *ground* of our salvation is the blood of Jesus, which is the blood of the covenant. We are saved because of the death of Jesus on the cross. But the *means* of our salvation is faith. We enter into a good relationship with God through faith in Christ.

Law

In the Old Testament the Mosaic law was given to regulate the lives of the members of the covenant. "The law is the instrument of the covenant. . . . It demands absolute trust and obedience."[3]

The law is like a marriage contract. We get married out of love, not because of the law. But the marriage contract is a law that reminds us to be faithful to our husband or wife.

The law reminds us to be faithful to God alone: "You shall have no other gods before me" (Ex 20:3). "Love Yahweh your God with all your heart and with all your soul and with all your strength" (Deut 6:5).

The law also tells us to live a holy life. We should not murder, commit adultery, steal, lie or covet (Ex 20:13-17). We should love our neighbor and have compassion on the poor and the alien (Lev 19:18,10).

The summary of the law, according to Jesus, is to love God and to love our neighbor (Mt 22:37-40).

So the primary function of the law is to guide the believer in his or her life. The law guided the Old Testament believers in their lives; the law guides the New Testament believers in their lives.

This is the positive, moral use of the law. John Calvin calls this the "principal use of the law."[4] John Wesley says that we establish the law "when we preach faith in Christ [to] produce holiness."[5]

But the apostle Paul also recognized a negative use of the law. The law shows us that we are sinful and under the judgment of God. Paul

---

[3]H. Berkhof, *Christian Faith*, p. 236.
[4]J. Calvin, *Institutes of the Christian Religion* 2.7.12 (p. 360).
[5]J. Wesley, "The Law Established through Faith, II," in *The Works of John Wesley*, 5:462,

wrote: "no one will be declared righteous in [God's] sight by observing the law; rather, through the law we become conscious of sin" (Rom 3:20).

Martin Luther experienced the judgment of the law in his life. Luther said: "The law brings the wrath of God, kills, reviles, accuses, judges and condemns everything that is not in Christ."[6] In other words, the law condemns us and drives us to seek salvation in Jesus Christ. This is the negative use of the law. But the result of this condemnation can be positive: if we are condemned by the law then we may run to Christ for salvation.

Yet Luther also recognized the positive function of the law. His *Large* and *Small Catechisms* contain instructions on the relevance of the Ten Commandments for the Christian.

And John Calvin recognized the negative function of the law. He said that the law condemns all people so that "naked and empty-handed, they flee to [God's] mercy, repose entirely in it [and] hide deep within it . . . . God's mercy is revealed in Christ to all who seek and wait upon it with true faith."[7]

Wesley also taught that the law convinces the world of sin and slays the sinner "to bring him unto life, unto Christ, that he may live."[8] Thus this so-called negative function is actually positive since it brings the sinner to Christ.

---

[6]M. Luther, "Heidelberg Disputation," in *Luther's Works* 31:54.

[7]J. Calvin, *Institutes of the Christian Religion*, 2.7.8 (p. 357).

[8]J. Wesley, "The Origin, Nature, Property, and Use of the Law," in *The Works of John Wesley* 5:442-43.

Study Questions

1. How is an unconditional, unilateral covenant an act of grace?
2. What is the purpose of the Sinaitic and new covenants?
3. Explain the negative function of the law. Is this function really negative?
4. Explain the positive function of the law.
5. **Essay:** How does the Christian view of the law differ from the Muslim view of the law?

CHAPTER 12

THE PERSON OF CHRIST

Once Jesus asked his disciples, "Who do people say I am?" Then he asked, "Who do you say I am?" (Mk 8:27-29). This is the topic of christology, or the person of Christ. Who is Jesus of Nazareth?

The New Testament often uses metaphors to answer this question: Jesus is "the bread of life," "the light of the world," "the gate for the sheep," "the good shepherd," "the resurrection and the life," and "the way and the truth and the life" (Jn 6:35; 9:5; 10:7,11; 11:25; 14:6).

African Christian theology often uses contexualized metaphors in its christology. These metaphors or images frequently describe functions of Jesus Christ.

Often in Africa Jesus is pictured as a Chief or as a King. The Ghanaian theologian John Pobee wrote: "In our Akan Christology we propose to think of Jesus as the *okyeame*, or linguist, who in all public matters was as the Chief, God, and is the first officer of the state, in this case the world."[1]

---

[1] J. Pobee, *Toward an African Theology* (Nashville: Abingdon, 1979), p. 95.

François Kabasélé from Congo speaks of Christ as chief.[2] Douglas Waruta from Kenya sees Jesus as potentate or king, as well as being a prophet and a priest.[3]

Other African theologians see Jesus as healer. Cécé Kolié from Guinea sees Jesus as a healer in the African context.[4] Kofi Appiah-Kubi from Ghana portrays Jesus as mediator, savior, liberator and healer.[5]

Others have seen Jesus as an elder brother. Harry Sawyerr prefers the concept of elder brother to that of chief. African chiefs are not readily accessible to the ordinary person. But the elder brother is accessible.[6]

The most controversial African title given to Jesus is that of ancestor. John Pobee wrote: "Our approach would be to look on Jesus as the Great and Greatest Ancestor—in the Akan language *Nana*."[7] Charles Nyamiti agrees: "the Redeemer shines forth as THE Brother-Ancestor par excellence, of whom the African ancestors are but faint and poor images."[8] Bénézet Bujo wants to give Jesus the title of "Ancestor Par Excellence" or "Proto-Ancestor."[9]

But is Jesus really an ancestor in the African sense? Tersur Aben observes that "African traditional religions never predicate the term ancestor of a deity. . . . Ancestor can be predicated rightly of deceased

[2]F. Kabasélé, "Christ as Chief," in *Faces of Jesus in Africa* (Maryknoll: Orbis, 1991), pp. 103-15.
[3]D. Waruta, "Who is Jesus Christ for Africans Today? Prophet, Priest, Potentate," in *Faces of Jesus in Africa*, pp. 52-64.
[4]C. Kolié, "Jesus as Healer?" in *Faces of Jesus in Africa*, pp. 128-50.
[5]K. Appiah-Kubi, "Christology," in *A Reader in African Christian Theology* (London: SPCK, 1997), pp. 65-74.
[6]H. Sawyerr, *Creative Evangelism* (London: Lutterworth, 1968), pp. 72-73.
[7]J. Pobee, *Toward an African Theology*, p. 94.
[8]C. Nyamiti, *Christ as our Ancestor* (Gweru: Mambo Press, 1984), p. 70.
[9]B. Bujo, *African Theology in its Social Context* (Nairobi: Paulines, 1992), p. 72.

human persons, but it cannot be rightly predicated of the living Son of God."[10]

Ole Ronkiei, a Kenyan layman, said: "Christ can't be an ancestor! No! How can he be? He was a young kid! . . . He didn't have a wife! He didn't have children! Where are the offspring?"[11] A Ugandan Catholic sister, Mary John, said that Jesus is not her ancestor "because he is not of my tribe. The ancestors of Buganda must have been the Baganda—only."[12]

Many—but not all—of the metaphors or titles listed above are useful in understanding who Jesus is. So what are some of the biblical titles for Jesus?

In the first place, he had a personal name, Jesus. His name is like the name of Joshua in the Old Testament. Jesus means Savior. The angel told Joseph to call him Jesus "because he will save his people from their sins" (Mt 1:21).

During his ministry it became evident that Jesus was the promised Messiah. At Caesarea Philippi, Peter confessed that Jesus was the Messiah or Christ (Mk 8:29). *Mashiah* is the Hebrew word for the anointed one or Messiah; *Christos* is the Greek translation. So Christ means that Jesus is the promised Messiah.

In the Gospels, Christ is usually a title, meaning that Jesus is the Messiah. But after Jesus' resurrection, he was called Jesus Christ. Then Christ became a second personal name of the Messiah. This is particularly clear in Paul's writings (see, for example, Rom. 1:1,4,6,7,8 etc.).

---

[10]T. Aben, *African Christian Theology*, pp. 128-29.

[11]Quoted in D. Stinton, *Jesus of Africa* (Nairobi: Paulines, 2004), p. 155.

[12]Quoted in D. Stinton, *Jesus of Africa*, p. 154.

The divinity of Jesus

During and after his ministry on earth, it became clear that Jesus was not only human but that he was also divine. This is clear throughout the New Testament.

The Synoptic Gospels record the words of God the Father during Jesus' baptism and transfiguration that Jesus is God's Son (Mt 3:17; 17:5; par.).[13] Matthew gives us Peter's confession as, "You are the Messiah, the Son of the living God" (Mt 16:16). Even Satan and the demons knew that Jesus was God. Twice Satan called Jesus the Son of God (Mt 4:3,6; par.). Once an evil spirit cried out in fear, "I know who you are—the Holy One of God!" (Mk 1:24). At the crucifixion, the centurion concluded, "Surely he was the Son of God!" (Mt 27:54, par.).

John's testimony to the divinity of Jesus is strong. His gospel begins with the statement that "the Word was with God and the Word was God." This Word "became flesh and lived among us" (Jn 1:1,14). Jesus said that "before Abraham was born, I am" (Jn 8:58). When Jesus said that "I and the Father are one," the Jews rightly concluded that Jesus claimed to be God (Jn 10:30-33). At the end of the Gospel, Thomas said to Jesus, "My Lord and my God!" (Jn 20:28).

The apostle Paul agreed with the testimony of the Gospels. Paul said that although Jesus was "in the form of God," he "did not consider equality with God something to be grasped" (Phil 2:6). Paul says Jesus is "the image of the invisible God" and "in Christ all the fullness of the Deity lives in bodily form" (Col 1:15; 2:9).

The author of Hebrews says that "the Son is the radiance of God's glory and the exact representation of his being" (Heb 1:3).

---

[13]"Par." refers to parallel Synoptic texts.

These and other places in the New Testament tell us that Jesus was indeed divine. But human reason objects. How can God become human?

Paul of Samosata, bishop of Antioch from 260 to 272, believed that Jesus was only a man who was filled with the power of God. The early church rejected this view because they believed that Jesus was more than an ordinary man.

Arius was a presbyter from Alexandria in Egypt. Arius said that the Son or the Word was the creator of the world but that he was not fully God. "There was a time when the Word was not," said Arius.

But the Council of Nicea in 325 said that the pre-existent Son is of the same essence (*homo-ousios*) as the Father. Jesus is fully divine.

For Athanasius, the young theologian at Nicea, the divinity of Jesus is important. If Jesus is not fully divine, how then could Jesus pay for the sins of the entire world? Our salvation depends on the divinity of Christ.

In our modern times, liberalism denies Christ's divinity. But the global evangelical movement affirms this historic truth.

The humanity of Jesus

It should be obvious that Jesus was fully human. John said that the Word "became flesh" and lived among us (Jn 1:14). Jesus was born of a human mother in Bethlehem. The child Jesus "grew and became strong"; he "grew in wisdom and stature" (Lk 2:40,52).

In the wilderness Jesus was hungry (Mt 4:2, par.); in Sychar he asked a woman for a drink (Jn 4:7); on the cross he was thirsty (Jn 19:28). After his death, blood and water came from his side (Jn 19:34).

The author of Hebrews affirms the humanity of Christ: "Since the children have flesh and blood, he too shared in their humanity . . . . [He] had to be made like his brothers in every way" (Heb 2:14,17).

Gnosticism and pre-Gnosticism thought that Jesus was divine but not human. The apostle John wrote against this heresy: "Many deceivers, who do not acknowledge Jesus Christ as coming in the flesh, have gone out into the world. Any such person is the deceiver and the antichrist" (2 Jn 1:7).

The church fathers knew that for Jesus to be a complete Savior, he would have to be fully human and fully divine. Only a human being can make sacrifice for other humans; only God can make sacrifice for all of humanity.

One person with two natures

So if Jesus is both God and man, is he one person or two persons?

Nestorius was a theologian who is thought to have said that Jesus had two persons. (Whether Nestorius actually said this is not certain.) But this theology would contradict the unity of Christ.

On the other hand, Eutyches is thought to have said that Jesus had one mixed divine-human nature. (Eutyches' position is *monophysite*, meaning "one nature." The Coptic Church in Egypt is Monophysite.)

But how can the divinity of God be mixed with the humanity of man? God is God, and man is man! They cannot be mixed.

In 451 the early church held a council at Chalcedon. This council concluded that Jesus is one person with two natures: a divine nature and a human nature. These two natures are not confused, not changeable, not divisible and not separable. They are distinct natures that cannot be separated or mixed.

This is the miracle of the incarnation. At the right time God humbled himself and became man. The incarnation and the cross reveal a God who is radically different from the God of natural theology. The God of natural theology is exalted; the God revealed in Jesus Christ is not only high but also one who comes down to be near us.

Study Questions

1. What is the meaning of Jesus and Christ?
2. What was Arius' view of the person of Christ? What was the response of the Council of Nicea?
3. What did Gnosticism teach about Jesus? What was the apostle John's response to pre-Gnosticism?
4. Why is it important that Jesus be both fully divine and fully human?
5. What was the decision of the Council of Chalcedon?
6. What is the difference between the Christian and the Muslim view of Jesus Christ?
7. **Essay:** Write a contextualized essay on the person of Christ.

CHAPTER 13

THE WORK OF CHRIST

If Jesus is indeed God and man, why did Jesus come to this earth? As Anselm of Canterbury asked in the title of one of his books: *Why Did God Become Man?*

Historically and theologically there are three main answers to this question. There are three basic theories of the work of Christ.[1]

Moral influence theory

Some theologians have said that the main human problem is our lack of love. We need someone to come from heaven to teach us what love really is. We need someone to motivate us into a life of love.

So Jesus came from heaven to teach us about love. Jesus taught this through his words and through his life (and death). The Sermon on the Mount and Jesus' parables teach us about love. Jesus' ministry of healing expresses his compassion and love. Jesus' death on the cross is the supreme example of Jesus' love. This is the moral influence or moral example theory of the atonement.

This theory of the atonement corresponds to Jesus' office of prophet. According to this theory Jesus was a great prophet like Isaiah

---

[1]See J. Stott, *The Cross of Christ* (Downers Grove: IVP, 1986), pp. 165-251; G. Fackre, *The Christian Story* (Grand Rapids: Eerdmans, 1996), pp. 118-51.

or Jeremiah. Jesus was sent to the earth to tell us about God and God's expectations for us humans.

Peter Abelard (1079-1142) of France held to this theory. European liberalism is another example. Adolf von Harnack (1851-1930) was a German liberal who taught this theory. Even Islam teaches that Jesus is a great prophet.

There is truth in the moral example theory. But it would be wrong to reduce the work of Christ to just that of being a positive example. That would be reductionism. (Reductionism *reduces* a truth to just one aspect of the truth.) Surely the work of Christ is more than just teaching.

So the moral influence theory by itself is inadequate. It does not take human sin and guilt very seriously. It does not provide a solution to the problem of human sin.

We are guilty before God. Who will take away our guilt?

Satisfaction theory

The Bible speaks extensively of our human sin and guilt. The first part of the book of Romans is very clear on this issue: "The wrath of God is being revealed from heaven against all human godlessness and wickedness . . . . There is no one righteous, not even one . . . . All have sinned and fall short of the glory of God" (Rom 1:18; 3:10,23).

The satisfaction theory of the atonement teaches that God's holiness and justice demand that a punishment or satisfaction be made for the enormous sins of mankind. In this way God's holiness or justice is satisfied.

So who is able to make this payment? The answer is that only God can make the payment to satisfy God's own holiness. Only God is big enough to make the payment for the sins of the whole world.

This then is a paradox. The problem is God—God's holiness; the solution is God—God's love. God out of his love provided a solution for God's holiness.

The solution is Jesus Christ, who is fully God and fully man. For only God can pay for the sins of all mankind; and only a human can pay for the sins of other humans.

So Jesus was the sacrificial lamb who was sacrificed on the cross for our sins. Jesus was the ransom payment for our salvation. "Christ redeemed us from the curse of the law by becoming a curse for us" (Gal 3:13).

The satisfaction theory of the atonement has broad support in the New Testament. A few key terms stand out.

First is *propitiation*. Paul, in Romans 3:25, calls Jesus a "propitiation." (Some translations wrongly have "sacrifice of atonement" or "expiation.") A sacrifice of propitiation turns away the wrath of God (or the gods). The sacrifice of Jesus—remarkably—turns away the wrath of God because Jesus satisfied God's justice.

Second is *the blood of Jesus*. Paul says that we have salvation because of the blood of Jesus. We have propitiation, justification, redemption, reconciliation and peace through the blood of Jesus (Rom 3:25; 5:9; Eph 1:7; 2:13; Col 1:20). The book of Hebrews teaches that "without the shedding of blood there is no forgiveness" (Heb 9:22).

The blood of Jesus in the New Testament is not a magical means of protection. Instead the blood of Jesus denotes the sacrifice of Jesus.[2]

Redemption and *ransom* are terms from the commercial world. Redemption and ransom suggest that a price had to be paid for our sins. Jesus said that the Son of Man came "to give his life as a ransom [or payment] for many" (Mk 10:45).

---

[2]See T. Palmer, *A Theology of the New Testament* (Bukuru: Africa Christian Textbooks, 2012), chapter 15.

Justification is a term from the legal world. A believer is justified or declared righteous because of the death of Jesus on the cross. The gospel or good news is the "righteousness of God" (Rom 1:17; 3:21). This righteousness or justice consists in our being declared righteous or just because of the sacrifice of Jesus.

The doctrine of justification presupposes the substitutionary atonement. Jesus was our substitute on the cross. "God made him who had no sin to be sin for us, so that in him we might become the righteousness of God" (2 Cor 5:21). And, "Christ redeemed us from the curse of the law by becoming a curse for us" (Gal 3:13).

The satisfaction theory of the atonement teaches that Jesus satisfied the justice of God and therefore we are acquitted and just. This is the priestly office of Jesus: he was both the sacrifice and the priest, atoning for sin.

This theory was first taught by Anselm of Canterbury (1033-1109) in his book *Cur Deus Homo* (Why Did God Become Man?). The Reformers and the Evangelicals also taught this theory. This was Luther's great discovery; it was Calvin's teaching; and it is at the heart of Wesley's theology. This is the theology that is common in our hymns.

In his sermon "The Lord our Righteousness," John Wesley said that through Christ's death "our ransom [was] paid, and [God's] justice satisfied."[3]

Charles Wesley in his song "And Can It Be" sang,

> No condemnation now I dread;
> Jesus, and all in him, is mine.
> Alive in him, my living head,
> and clothed in righteousness divine,
> bold I approach the eternal throne,

---

[3]J. Wesley, "The Lord our Righteousness," in *The Works of John Wesley*, 5:239.

and claim the crown, through Christ my own![4]

Christus Victor theory

The Christus Victor theory of the atonement says that Jesus came to the earth to defeat Satan and the evil powers. ("Christus Victor" in Latin means "Christ Victorious.")

In his life and death and resurrection Jesus triumphed over Satan and the forces of evil. During his earthly ministry Jesus and his disciples often cast out demons. Once when his disciples had cast out many demons, Jesus said, "I saw Satan fall like lightening from heaven" (Lk 10:18).

But the decisive blow to Satan occurred at the cross. Just before his crucifixion Jesus said: "now the prince of this world will be driven out" (Jn 12:31). Paul said that "having disarmed the powers and authorities, [Jesus] made a public spectacle of them, triumphing over them by the cross" (Col 2:15).

So what happened on the cross? On the cross Jesus paid for our sins, and Satan then was defeated. Paul says: "The sting of death is sin, and the power of sin is the law. But thanks be to God who gives us the victory through our Lord Jesus Christ" (1 Cor 15:56-57). Jesus is the ultimate Victor over Satan through his work on the cross.

This theory was set forth by the Swedish theologian Gustav Aulen in 1931. In his book *Christus Victor*, Aulen shows how Christ's work on earth meant the defeat of the powers of evil. Unfortunately, though, Aulen puts his Christus Victor theory in opposition to the satisfaction theory. Obviously both theories are true. Christ defeated Satan decisively by paying for our sins.

---

[4]C. Wesley, "And Can It Be," in *The Methodist Hymnal* (Nashville: The Methodist Publishing House, 1964), #527.

This theory corresponds to the kingly office of Jesus. Jesus is both the suffering lamb and the royal lion (Rev 5:5-6). Therefore, "Worthy is the Lamb who was slain to receive power" (Rev 5:12).

This theory is very relevant to the African situation where evil spirits are a reality. Osadolor Imasogie says that we must have "a new appreciation of the efficacy of Christ's power over evil spiritual forces."[5]

Conclusion

So why did God become man? He became man to teach and show us the love of God; he became man in order to pay for our sins and justify us; and he became man in order to triumph over the powers of Satan. A full doctrine of the work of Christ will take all three of these aspects seriously.

Study Questions

1. What are the three offices of Christ? How do the three theories of the atonement correspond to these three offices?
2. Describe the moral influence theory of the atonement.
3. Describe the danger of reductionism of the moral influence theory.
4. What is propitiation? How is Jesus' death a propitiation?
5. Briefly describe the satisfaction theory of the atonement.
6. How are the views of Peter Abelard and Anselm of Canterbury different?
7. How did Jesus triumph over Satan?
8. **Essay:** Write an essay on the blood of Jesus in the theology of Paul. (Use a concordance.) Can we cover our cars with the blood of Jesus, according to Paul?

---

[5]O. Imasogie, *Guidelines for Christian Theology in Africa*, p. 79.

CHAPTER 14

SALVATION

Soteriology is the doctrine of salvation. Soteriology is the appropriation of the benefits of the work of Christ. So what is salvation in the theological sense?

Wholistic salvation

Early missionary theology tended to be individualistic and other-worldly. Salvation for these early missionaries was then the salvation of the soul, and not of the body. Salvation for them is the forgiveness of sins.

This individual dimension of salvation has some basis in Scripture. The Messiah is called Jesus "because he will save his people from their sins" (Mt 1:21). Jesus brought "salvation through the forgiveness of . . . sins" (Lk 1:77).

Peter said that salvation is found only through the name of Jesus (Acts 4:12). Paul told the Philippian jailor, "Believe in the Lord Jesus, and you will be saved" (Acts 16:31). Paul said that if one confesses Jesus as Lord and if one believes, he will be saved (Rom 10:9). Paul also said that "it is by grace you have been saved, through faith" (Eph 2:8).

Salvation in this context is equivalent to justification. Those who believe in Jesus are justified and saved; those who do not believe are not saved.

But liberation theology has reacted against this missionary theology by emphasizing the physical and social dimensions of salvation. But in so doing, liberation theology has often gone to the other extreme.

Gustavo Gutierrez is one of the founders of liberation theology. Gutierrez thinks we should not be talking of the quantity or number of those saved but rather of the quality of our salvation. Gutierrez says, "Salvation is not something otherworldly, in regard to which the present life is merely a test. Salvation . . . is something which embraces all human reality."[1] For him salvation is primarily a socio-economic-political liberation.

Allan Boesak complains about the older European commentaries that spiritualize Jesus' manifesto of liberation in Luke 4:18-19. Boesak says that "to spiritualize this reality is to invite heresy."[2] But then Boesak too goes to the other extreme of seeing salvation as a purely socio-economic-political liberation.

Liberation theology has done us a favor by reminding us of the physical dimension of salvation. But it has too often gone to the other extreme by rejecting the spiritual dimension of salvation.

A careful study of salvation in the Bible suggests that salvation is wholistic. It is salvation of both the body and the soul.

We see this, for example, in the exodus. God saved the Israelites not only from a physical bondage but also a spiritual bondage. The purpose of the exodus was not just socio-economic liberation but also spiritual

---

[1] G. Gutierrez, *A Theology of Liberation* (Maryknoll: Orbis, 1973), p. 151.
[2] A. Boesak, *Farewell to Innocence* (Maryknoll: Orbis, 1976), p. 25.

salvation. The goal of the exodus was Mount Sinai, where God made a covenant with his people.

The book of Luke also teaches wholistic salvation. Salvation is both deliverance from one's enemies and forgiveness of sins (Lk 1:71,77). Luke describes the wholistic salvation of many: a sinful woman (7:50), a demon-possessed man (8:36), a woman with bleeding (8:48), Jairus' daughter (8:50), a Samaritan leper (17:19), a blind beggar (18:42) and a corrupt tax collector (19:9-10).[3] Surely Jesus' message of salvation in Luke 4:18-19 should be understood wholistically.

The Kingdom of God

When Jesus began his ministry on earth, he proclaimed that "the kingdom of God is near" (Mk 1:15). The kingdom of God is the renewal of all of life by God through his Son Jesus. The kingdom of God is a wholistic redemptive concept.

The kingdom of God is the realm of salvation for those who believe in Jesus and whose sins are thereby forgiven. Only those who humble themselves like children can enter the kingdom of God (Mt 18:1-5).

But the kingdom of God also includes the redemption of physical and social life. When Jesus began his ministry, he preached the good news of the kingdom and he healed those who were sick (Mt 4:23). His disciples also preached the kingdom, healed the sick and cast out demons (Mt 10:7-8).

When John the Baptist asked if Jesus was the Messiah, Jesus said that the blind see, the lame walk, the lepers are cleansed, the deaf hear, the dead are raised, and good news is preached to the poor (Mt 11:4-5). The kingdom of God is indeed wholistic.

---

[3]The Greek word for save (*sōzō*) is used in most of these passages.

Salvation then means the restoration of the original creation. It begins by the renewal of the person. But it includes the renewal of all of God's creation. Salvation is wholistic in nature.

Study Questions

1.   What is soteriology?
2.   Evaluate liberation theology's view of salvation.
3.   Why did God liberate his people from Egypt?
4.   Describe the salvation in Jesus' manifesto in Luke 4:18-19.
5.   What is the precondition for salvation in the book of Acts?
6.   **Essay:** Write an essay on salvation in the book of Luke.

CHAPTER 15

~~~~~~

THE HOLY SPIRIT AND CHRISTIAN BEGINNINGS

Personal salvation occurs when a person believes in Jesus and is saved. Paul said to the Philippian jailor, "Believe in the Lord Jesus and you will be saved" (Acts 16:31).

But the question has been asked: how does a person believe? What or who is the final cause of a person's conversion? To what extent is the Holy Spirit a cause of a person's faith?

Historically two main answers have been given to these questions. Either the final cause is the Holy Spirit or the final cause is a human's will. We will consider these two positions.

The Augustinian view[1]

There is significant evidence in the Bible to support the view that God is the first and final cause of our salvation.

The doctrine of election says that God chose (or elected) believers from eternity. Paul said that God "chose us in [Christ] before the creation of the world." In Christ "we were also chosen, having been

---

[1] See T. Palmer, *The Reformed and Presbyterian Faith* (Bukuru: Africa Christian Textbooks, 2013), chapter 11, for a summary of Augustinianism.

predestined according to the plan of him who works out everything in conformity with the purpose of his will" (Eph 1:4,11).

Elsewhere Paul says: "For those God foreknew he also predestined to be conformed to the likeness of his Son" (Rom 8:29). Then he talks of "God's purpose in election" (Rom 9:11).

If a person is elected, then the Holy Spirit will change the person's heart. Jesus told Nicodemus that "the Spirit gives birth to spirit" and a believer is "born of the Spirit" (Jn 3:5-8). Jesus also said that "no one can come to me unless the Father who sent me draws him" (Jn 6:44).

Augustine, who came from North Africa, was a man who believed in election. (Augustinianism is the theology of Augustine.) As a young man Augustine lived a stubborn and sinful life. He consistently resisted the Gospel. But then he was converted, and he believed that it was God who converted him. Only God's grace was strong enough to convert such a stubborn man. Augustine tells his story in his *Confessions*.

Martin Luther also believed strongly in God's grace. In 1525 he wrote *The Bondage of the Will*. There he compares the human will to a horse. "If God rides it, it wills and goes where God wills." But, "if Satan rides it, it wills and goes where Satan wills."[2]

John Calvin also taught election and predestination. Calvin taught the sovereignty of God but also human responsibility. Election gives the believer comfort that God loves him or her. At the same time, a person is also responsible for his or her own actions.

The Synod of Dordrecht (1618-1619) affirmed its belief in election in response to the Dutch pastor Arminius. The five points of Calvinism were developed at the Synod of Dort. These five points of Calvinism are total depravity, unconditional election, limited atonement, irresistible grace and the perseverance of the saints.

---

[2]M. Luther, "The Bondage of the Will," in *Luther's Works* 33:65.

The Anglican *Thirty-Nine* Articles also speaks of election. This doctrine, it says, is "full of sweet, pleasant and unspeakable comfort to godly persons."[3]

Augustinianism teaches the "amazing grace" of God in the life of a believer.

The Arminian view

But election is difficult to understand. How can God choose some people and not others? Are we not ultimately responsible for our own salvation?

At the time of Augustine, a British monk named Pelagius rejected the doctrine of election and insisted on a person's freedom to choose for or against Jesus.

At the time of Luther, the humanist Erasmus wrote *The Freedom of the Will* arguing that the free offer of the Gospel implies that a person has the freedom of the will. The human person, not God, decides one's own salvation.

Some time later, a Dutch pastor called Arminius reaffirmed his belief in the free will of a person. Arminianism rejects the doctrine of irresistible grace and affirms the freedom of a person to finally choose for or against Christ.

John Wesley followed Arminius in his thinking. In 1740 he preached a sermon entitled "Free Grace." There he spoke of "the horrible decree of predestination."[4] For him the free offer of the Gospel to all means that the doctrines of election and predestination are not true. For him the elect are those whom God foreknew that they would believe.

---

[3]"The Thirty-Nine Articles of Religion," in *The Book of Common Prayer* (Abuja, 2007), p. 502.
[4]J. Wesley, "Free Grace," in *Wesley's Works* 7:383.

The Holy Spirit and salvation

The matter is not easy to resolve. One needs to listen carefully to the testimony of Scripture. One also needs to use one's reason, but realizing that one's reason too can lead a person astray.

Both positions agree that the Holy Spirit is active in the process of salvation. But which is stronger in the conversion process: the Holy Spirit or the human will? Augustinianism says that the Holy Spirit is stronger and that the Holy Spirit cannot be resisted; Arminianism says that the Holy Spirit can be resisted and that the human will makes the final decision.

But who can observe the workings of the Holy Spirit? Jesus said: "The wind blows wherever it pleases. You hear its sound, but you cannot tell where it comes from or where it is going. So it is with everyone born of the Spirit" (Jn 3:8). There remains a mystery in the work of God in the salvation of a person.

Study Questions

1. Why did St. Augustine become convinced of the doctrine of election?
2. Contrast the views of Erasmus and Luther on the human will.
3. Contrast the views of Arminius and the Synod of Dordrecht on election.
4. Is predestination a horrible doctrine? Read Romans 8:28-39.
5. **Essay:** Write an essay on your personal view of election.

CHAPTER 16

CONVERSION

The Bible tells us that every human person is sinful. Every person must trust or believe in Jesus Christ to receive salvation. In other words, we need to be converted.

The Bible gives us some stories of conversions. The most dramatic story is that of Saul (Paul). On the road to Damascus, Saul saw a bright light and heard the voice of Jesus. Saul was converted and became a disciple of Jesus (see Acts 9:1-9).

After Peter's speech at Pentecost, three thousand people repented and were baptized (Acts 2:38-41). The Philippian jailor was converted when he believed and was saved (Acts 16:31-33). Lydia was converted when the Lord opened her heart and she believed (Acts 16:14-15).

There are three important terms that describe the process of conversion: conversion itself, repentance and faith.

Conversion

The Greek word for conversion (*epistrophē*) is found only once in the Bible: at the council in Jerusalem Paul spoke of "the conversion of the Gentiles" (Acts 15:3; KJV).

The Greek verb (*epistrephō*) is more frequent. Literally, *epistrephō* means to turn or to convert. There are two sides to this turning or converting: one turns away from sin or idolatry, and one turns to Jesus Christ.

Jesus commissioned Paul to turn the Gentiles "from darkness to light and from the power of Satan to God" (Acts 26:18). Paul told the people at Lystra to turn from idols to the living God (Act 14:15). The Thessalonians "turned to God from idols" (1 Thess 1:9).

Conversion can then be defined as "the act of turning from one's sin in repentance and turning to Christ in faith."[1] Conversion then has two parts: repentance and faith. In conversion we turn away from sin in repentance, and we turn towards Jesus Christ in faith.

As we look at Scripture and church history, we observe a great variety of conversion patterns.[2] Some conversions are sudden; others are gradual. People convert for different reasons: out of fear of hell, because of an evangelistic sermon or through long and patient study of Scripture.

The conversions of Saul (Paul) and the Philippian jailor were sudden. St. Augustine was converted after a long period of intellectual and emotional wrestling and reflection. Martin Luther too wrestled with God and the Scriptures before he gradually saw the light. John Calvin speaks of a "sudden conversion" in his life.

But for many, conversion is a gradual process. This is especially true of children of believers who grow up in a Christian family and church. Gradually they come to a saving knowledge of Jesus Christ.

But in all cases, conversion is a turning away from sin and a turning to Jesus Christ.

---

[1] M. Erickson, *Christian Theology*, pp. 933-34.
[2] See A. Hoekema, *Saved by Grace* (Grand Rapids: Eerdmans, 1989), pp. 117-20.

Repentance

Repentance is closely related to conversion. In the Greek, repentance (*metanoia*) suggests a change of mind. "Repentance consists essentially in change of heart and mind and will."[3] Like conversion it has the sense of turning.

Both John the Baptist and Jesus began their ministry with the words, "Repent, for the kingdom of heaven is near" (Mt 3:2; 4:17). At the time of Jonah, Nineveh repented; but towns in Galilee refused to repent (Mt 12:41; 11:20). Yet there is rejoicing in heaven over one sinner who repents (Lk 15:7,10).

At Pentecost Peter called on the people to "repent and be baptized" (Acts 2:38). Again, Peter called on the people to "repent and turn to God" (Acts 3:19). Paul too preached that people "should repent and turn to God" (Acts 26:20).

Repentance sometimes refers to the beginning of one's salvation. But one's entire life should be a life of repentance. The first of Luther's *Ninety-five Theses* reads: "When our Lord and Master Jesus Christ said, 'Repent,' he willed the entire life of believers to be one of repentance."[4]

We see this frequently in the Old Testament. Frequently the prophets called on God's people to turn back (*shuv*) to God. God said to Solomon, "If my people . . . will turn from their wicked ways, then I will hear from heaven and forgive their sin and will heal their land" (2 Chr 7:14). At the time of Jeremiah, God said: "Return, faithless people, for I am your husband" (Jer 3:14).

The Christian life requires repeated sorrow and repentance for our sins.

---

[3]J. Murray, *Redemption—Accomplished and Applied* (Grand Rapids: Eerdmans, 1955), p. 114.

[4]M. Luther, "Ninety-five Theses," in *Luther's Works* 31:25.

Faith

If repentance has the sense of turning away from sin, faith has the positive sense of trusting in Jesus. Christian conversion is both turning away from sin and turning to God.

The Greek word for faith is *pistis*; the verb *pisteuō* means to have faith or to believe. Faith or belief has at least two parts.[5] First, faith means accepting a statement or proposition as being true. For example, we believe that God exists. This is our belief. Well, "good! Even the demons believe that—and shudder" (Jas 2:19). Here faith is agreement with a statement or fact.

Faith accepts the truth of other facts of the Christian message. Paul, quoting Isaiah, asks: "Who has believed our message?" (Rom 10:16). The Gentiles believed the message (*logos*) of the Gospel (Acts 15:7). John wrote his Gospel so that we may believe that Jesus is the Messiah, the Son of God (Jn 20:31).

So faith is assent or agreement to a fact. But saving faith is more than that. Saving faith is also personal trust in God or in Jesus Christ.

John 3:16 says: "whoever believes *in* him shall not perish but have eternal life." The preposition "in" suggests a personal trust in Jesus. Saving faith is not just agreement to a proposition; saving faith is trust *in* the person of Jesus.

John Murray writes: "Faith, after all, is not belief of propositions of truth respecting the Saviour . . . . Faith is trust in a person, the person of Christ, the Son of God and Saviour of the lost. It is entrustment of ourselves to him."[6]

This saving faith brings salvation. At Pentecost, Peter said: "Everyone who calls on the name of the Lord will be saved" (Acts

---

[5]M. Erickson, *Christian Theology*, p. 939.
[6]J. Murray, *Redemption—Accomplished and Applied*, pp. 111-12.

2:21). When Cornelius believed, he and his household were saved (Acts 11:14). The Philippian jailor was saved when he believed (Acts 16:30-31).

Paul says that justification or salvation comes through faith: "If you confess with you mouth, 'Jesus is Lord,' and believe in your heart that God raised him from the dead, you will be saved" (Rom 10:9). Again, "it is by grace you have been saved, through faith" (Eph 2:8).

Salvation comes through faith in Jesus Christ.

Study Questions

1. Define conversion.
2. Give three examples of Christian conversion.
3. Define repentance. Is it a single event or a process?
4. What are the two parts to faith?
5. **Essay:** Write an essay on conversion in the book of Acts.

CHAPTER 17

UNION WITH CHRIST

Faith is the means whereby we are saved. Faith brings justification and salvation to the believer. But faith also creates a new relationship with God for the believer. Through faith we become one with Christ.

A covenant of love

The purpose of the Old Testament covenants was to create a relationship of love between God and the believer. Out of love God entered into a covenant with Abraham and his family. Out of love God entered into a covenant with Israel at Mount Sinai.

Jeremiah and Hosea compare this covenant relationship to marriage. God said to Israel, "I remember the devotion of your youth, how as a bride you loved me and followed me through the desert" (Jer 2:2). In the Sinai desert God got married to Israel!

But Israel became a prostitute. Their idolatry was spiritual adultery. Yet God continued to love them. He told Hosea to marry a prostitute to show that God still loved the prostitute Israel. God said to Israel, "I will betroth you to me forever . . . . I will betroth you in faithfulness, and you will acknowledge Yahweh" (Hos 2:19-20).

God loved his people, and God expected that his people would love him in return. This is the essence of a covenant or relationship of love.

The New Testament gives a christological dimension to this relationship. We are not only one with God: we are also one with Jesus Christ. We are not only married to God: we are also married to Jesus Christ.

Paul says that the church is the bride of Jesus. He compares the relationship between Christ and his church to the relationship between a man and a woman. He says that the union between Jesus and the church is "a profound mystery" (Eph 5:32).

Martin Luther said that an incomparable benefit of faith is that "it unites the soul with Christ as a bride is united with her bridegroom." Faith is a "wedding ring" that leads to a "royal marriage." He continues: "Here this rich and divine bridegroom Christ marries this poor, wicked harlot, redeems her from all her evil, and adorns her with all his goodness."[1]

In Christ

A common phrase to designate this new relationship is "in Christ."[2] Our entire Christian existence is in Christ.

A Christian is chosen "in him" (Eph 1:4,11). Justification is "in Christ" (Gal 2:17). There is no condemnation for those "in Christ" (Rom 8:1). Believers are sanctified "in Christ Jesus" (1 Cor 1:2). Believers may die "in Christ" (1 Thess 4:16), and they will all be made alive "in Christ" (1 Cor 15:22).

The church is in Christ. The believers in Philippi are "in Christ Jesus" (Phil 1:1). The believers in Ephesus are "the faithful in Christ Jesus" (Eph 1:1) as are the believers in Colossae (Col 1:2). All believers are "one in Christ Jesus" since they "belong to Christ" (Gal 3:28-29).

---

[1] M. Luther, "The Freedom of a Christian," in *Luther's Works* 31:351-52.
[2] See L. Smedes, *All Things Made New* (Grand Rapids: Eerdmans, 1970), pp. 78-81.

The believer is in Christ. Paul says that "if anyone is in Christ, he is a new creation" (2 Cor 5:17). Paul desires to "be found in him" (Phil 3:9). A believer's life is "now hidden with Christ in God" (Col 3:3).

So how are we in Christ? The phrase "in Christ" suggests first of all that a person has identified with Jesus Christ through faith. If we believe in Christ, we have died and we have been raised with Christ. Paul says that a believer has "been united with [Christ] in his death" and "will certainly also be united with him in his resurrection" (Rom 6:5). In other words, through faith we "died with Christ" and we have been "raised with Christ" (Col 2:20; 3:1).

Being "in Christ" thus means being in a state of salvation. A person who is "in Christ" is a person who is saved. But being "in Christ" is more than that. Being "in Christ" suggests a relationship. A person who is "in Christ" is in a personal, spiritual relationship with Christ. This relationship is sometimes called a mystical relationship.

John's Gospel profoundly describes this relationship. Jesus is like a vine, and the believers are the branches. Therefore the believer should remain or abide in Christ (Jn 15:4,5,7). When a believer is in Christ, then Christ lives in the believer. "Remain (abide) in me, and I will remain (abide) in you," Jesus says (Jn 15:4; cf. vs. 5).

John Murray says that the union of the believer with Christ "is compared to the union which exists between the persons of the trinity in the Godhead. This is staggering, but it is the case."[3]

We find this in Jesus' high priestly prayer. Jesus prays that the believers will be one just as the Father is in Christ and Christ in the Father. Jesus continues, "May they also be in us" (Jn 17:20-21).

So how are we in Christ? What kind of mysticism is this? The key to this Christ-mysticism is the Holy Spirit. Through the Holy Spirit we are in Christ. Through prayer and meditation through the Holy Spirit,

[3] J. Murray, *Redemption—Accomplished and Applied*, p. 168.

we are one with Christ. John Calvin says that "the Holy Spirit is the bond by which Christ effectually unites us to himself."[4]

Christ in the believer

If a person believes in Jesus, this person is in Christ. But Christ also lives in this believer.

Not only should we abide in Christ, but Christ will abide in us. "Remain (abide) in me, and I will remain (abide) in you. . . . If a person remains (abides) in me and I in him, he will bear much fruit" (Jn 15:4-5).

Paul says that "I have been crucified with Christ and I no longer live, but Christ lives in me" (Gal 2:20). Paul also asks the Corinthians, "Do you not realize that Christ Jesus is in you?" (2 Cor 13:5).

So how is Christ in the believer? As God, Christ is omnipresent and thus also in the believer. But Paul also tells us that "the Lord is the Spirit" (2 Cor 3:17). Somehow, Jesus Christ is the Holy Spirit.

This is a trinitarian mystery. We have seen that there is a oneness in the Trinity as well as a threeness. So where the Son is, the Spirit is also present.

When Jesus ascended into heaven, he sent the Holy Spirit to be the Comforter and Counselor for the church. Jesus said, "You know him, for he lives with you and will be in you" (Jn 14:17).

It is the special role of the Holy Spirit to be the bond of union between Christ and the believer.

John Murray says that "union with Christ is the central truth of the whole doctrine of salvation. . . . Here indeed is mysticism on the highest plane. . . . It is the mysticism of communion with the one true and living God."[5]

---

[4] J. Calvin, *Institutes of the Christian Religion*, 3.1.1. (p. 538).
[5] J. Murray, *Redemption—Accomplished and Applied*, pp. 170, 172.

Words cannot adequately convey this mystical oneness. This union with God is cultivated by prayer and meditation. But it is the central reality of the doctrine of salvation.

Study Questions

1.   Describe the relationship that the Sinai covenant established.
2.   Describe Hosea's perspective on this relationship.
3.   How have we died and risen with Christ?
4.   How is a believer in Christ?
5.   How is Christ in the believer?
6.   **Essay:** Write an essay on what it means for you to be one with Christ.

CHAPTER 18

JUSTIFICATION AND SANCTIFICATION

The human problem is that we are not righteous (just) or holy. "There is no one righteous, not even one" (Rom 3:10). "All have sinned and fall short of the glory of God" (Rom 3:23).

So how can we be become just or holy? We become just or holy through faith. But there are two dimensions to the process of becoming just or holy: justification and sanctification. Justification is the legal declaration that we are just or holy; sanctification is the actual process of becoming holy.

Justification

We have seen that every human person is guilty because of his or her sins and is under God's wrath. But the good news is that God justifies us or makes us just. How then does God make us just?

The Roman Catholic Church said that justification is both a legal declaration of righteousness and the process whereby one actually becomes righteous. In other words, for them it is justification by faith and by works. Faith acquits a person before the Judge; works make a person holy in his or her life.

But the question can then be asked: how many works do we need to be justified? Justification is then based on our righteousness. But what if we are not good enough?

Martin Luther's great discovery was that a person is justified only through faith and not through good works. In other words, justification is the Judge's declaration of our innocence and righteousness. We are innocent by faith alone and not by our works.

The context of justification is the court room. God is the Judge; we who are guilty stand before the Judge. But Jesus bore the curse that was ours. Jesus was punished for us with the result that we are no longer guilty.

Paul writes: "Christ redeemed us from the curse of the law by becoming a curse for us" (Gal 3:13). And, "God made him who had no sin to be sin for us so that in him we might become the righteousness of God" (2 Cor 5:21).

The result is twofold: our sins are forgiven, and we are now declared righteous. Before the Judge, we are acquitted of our sins; and the Judge declares us righteous.

The *ground* of our justification, then, is the death of Jesus. Jesus died on the cross to pay for our sins. Jesus died to make us righteous. John Wesley writes: "the righteousness of Christ, both his active and passive righteousness, is the meritorious cause of our justification."[1]

The *process* of justification is imputation. This is the process whereby the righteousness of Christ is credited to the believer. Imputation is taught in Romans 4. There we learn that Abraham believed, and it was credited to him as righteousness. This is also true for the Christian—"for us, to whom God will credit righteousness" (Rom 4:23-24). Imputation is the process whereby Christ's righteousness is credited to the believer.

---

[1] J. Wesley, "The Lord our Righteousness," in *The Works of John Wesley*, 5:240.

John Wesley continues, "If we take the phrase of imputing Christ's righteousness for the bestowing (as it were) the righteousness of Christ . . . a believer may be said to be justified by the righteousness of Christ imputed."[2]

The *means* of justification is faith. Paul is absolutely clear on this. "We maintain that a person is justified by faith apart from works of law" (Rom 3:28). This is important, "for if righteousness could be gained through the law, Christ died for nothing" (Gal 2:21).

We are justified by faith, not by works. This then means that our justification is a legal or forensic declaration of righteousness, not the actual process of becoming holy. The Judge has acquitted us and declared us righteous.

The *result* of justification is our salvation. "Who will bring any charge against those whom God has chosen? It is God who justifies. Who is he that condemns?" (Rom 8:33-34).

After Luther discovered the doctrine of justification by faith alone, he exclaimed, "I felt that I was altogether born again and had entered paradise itself through open gates."[3] It was no longer necessary for one to accumulate enough good works to enter heaven.

Charles Wesley expressed the joy of justification in his song "And Can It Be." He sang,

> I woke,
> the dungeon flamed with light;
> my chains fell off,
> my heart was free,
> I rose, went forth and followed thee.[4]

---

[2]J. Wesley, "The Lord our Righteousness," p. 240.

[3]M. Luther, "Preface to the Complete Edition of Luther's Latin Writings," in *Luther's Works* 34:337.

[4]C. Wesley, "And Can It Be," in *The Methodist Hymnal*, #527.

Sanctification

Justification is the legal declaration of one's righteousness; sanctification, as commonly understood, is the process of making a person holy in his or her life.

Literally, the word "sanctify" means to make holy. Sometimes in the New Testament, sanctify means to consecrate, which is similar to justify (see Heb 10:10,29; 1 Cor 1:2; 6:11). But often sanctify or sanctification is the process whereby a person becomes holy in his or her life.

In systematic theology, sanctification is usually understood as the process of becoming holy in one's life. Sanctification is both the work of God and the believer in the Christian life.

The source of sanctification is our union with Christ. Bishop Ryle says: "Sanctification . . . is the invariable result of that vital union with Christ which true faith gives to a person." As Jesus said: "The one who remains in me, and I in him, bears much fruit" (Jn 15:5).[5] If we are one with Christ, we will be a new creature and we will live a life of holiness.

Scripture tells us that it is God who sanctifies the believer. Paul prays, "May God himself, the God of peace, sanctify you through and through" (1 Thess 5:23). Especially it is God the Holy Spirit who sanctifies a person. The believers in Thessalonica were chosen "to be saved through the sanctifying work of the Spirit" (2 Thess 2:13).

A primary work of the Holy Spirit is sanctification. The Holy Spirit regenerates a new believer and makes the believer into a new creation. Then the Holy Spirit progressively works in the life of a believer. Sanctification is the process of becoming holy.

Sanctification is both the work of God and of us humans. Paul tells the Philippian believers "to work out your own salvation with fear and

---

[5] J. C. Ryle, *Holiness* (Ibadan: Amazing Grace, 1994), p. 17.

trembling, for it is God who works in you" (Phil 2:12-13). Paradoxically, in this text it is both God and the believer who acts or works.

Sanctification then is also the work of the believer. The believer is to "work out [one's] salvation with fear and trembling" (Phil 2:12). Believers should offer their bodies "in slavery to righteousness leading to holiness" (Rom 6:19).

Holiness is the essence of sanctification. God calls us to be holy: "Be holy, because I am holy" (1 Pet 1:16). Paul writes to the Thessalonian believers: "It is God's will that you should be holy . . . . God did not call us to be impure but to live a holy life" (1 Thess 4:3,7).

Scripture is full of calls to holiness. The New Testament epistles, for example, frequently start with a doctrinal section and conclude with a practical call to holiness. The final section of Romans begins with: "Therefore, I urge you . . . to offer your bodies as living sacrifices, holy and pleasing to God" (Rom 12:1). The second half of Colossians begins with a call to "set your hearts on things above" (Col 3:1). The second half of Ephesians begins with a call "to live a life worthy of the calling you have received" (Eph 4:1).

It is clear from Scripture that sanctification is a process. Bishop Ryle writes: "Justification is a finished and complete work . . . . Sanctification is an imperfect work, comparatively, and will never be perfected until we reach heaven."[6]

Sanctification is the process of being "conformed to the likeness of [God's] Son" (Rom 8:29). Sanctification is the process of becoming perfect. Jesus once said, "Be perfect, therefore, as your heavenly Father is perfect" (Matt 5:48).

But will perfection be attained on earth? John Wesley thought so. He thought that the command to be perfect implied the ability to attain

---

[6]J.C. Ryle, *Holiness*, p. 29.

to perfection in this life.[7] But other non-Wesleyan theologians think that the pollution of sin is too extensive to allow for perfection in this life.

Yet the goal of perfection stands for every sincere Christian. Every Christian must strive to be like Christ in every aspect of his or her being.

Just and holy

Justification and sanctification are the two sides of the Christian life. A Christian is just or righteous before God's law; and a Christian strives for holiness in his or her life.

Without Jesus we are not just or holy. But through faith in Jesus we become one with Jesus Christ. Then through Christ and his Spirit we become legally (forensically) just and we are becoming holy in our lives. (See diagram on justification and sanctification.)

---

[7]See J. Wesley, "A Plain Account of Christian Perfection" in *The Works of John Wesley* 11:366-446.

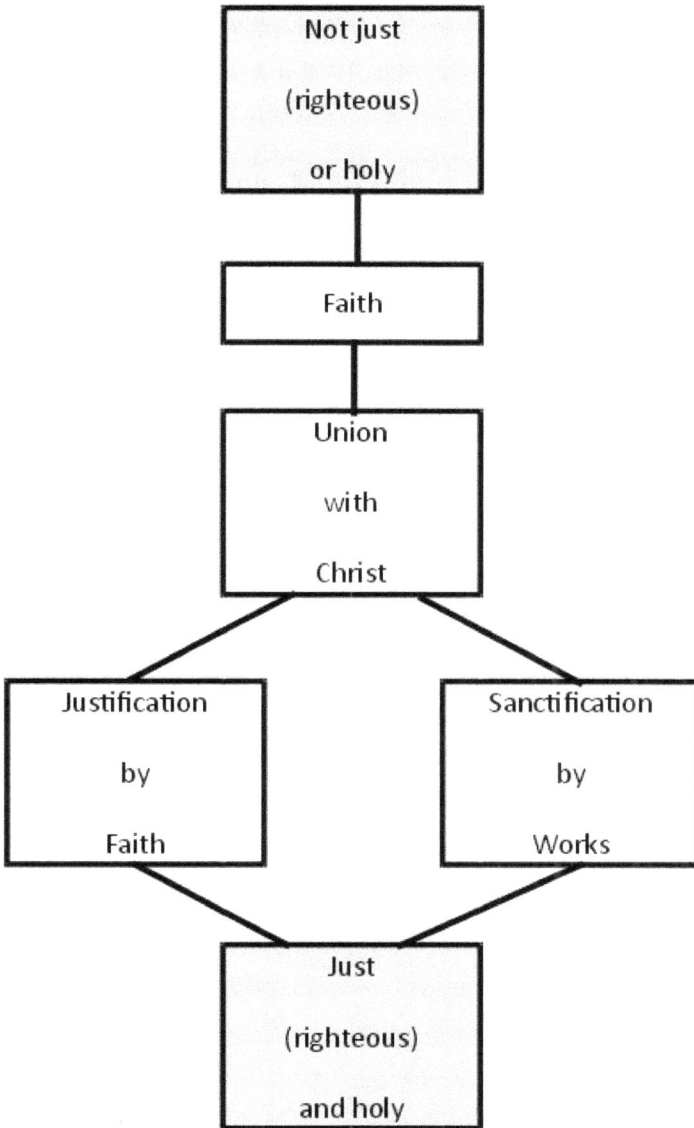

Figure 1: Diagram on Justification and Sanctification

But what if a person claims to have faith in Jesus but does not have good works? James is clear on this: "Faith by itself, if it has no works, is dead" (Jas 2:17). Then James makes the intriguing statement: "You see that a person is justified by works and not by faith alone" (Jas 2:24).

The intention of James is clear. *We are justified by a living faith that produces good works.* We are not justified by a dead faith that does not produce good works. Good works and holiness are an integral part of the Christian life.

Jesus once said: "Every good tree bears good fruit, but a bad tree bears bad fruit. A good tree cannot bear bad fruit, and a bad tree cannot bear good fruit. Every tree that does not bear good fruit is cut down and thrown into the fire. Thus by their fruit you will know them" (Mt 7:17-20).

If a person believes in Jesus and is filled with the Holy Spirit, that person will live a life of holiness.

Study Questions

1. What is the difference between the Roman Catholic and the Protestant understanding of justification?
2. What are the ground and means of justification?
3. Describe the doctrine of imputation.
4. Compare and contrast justification and sanctification.
5. Do you think Christian perfection is possible in this life? Explain.
6. **Essay:** Compare Paul's and James' theology of justification by faith.

CHAPTER 19

THE HOLY SPIRIT AND THE CHRISTIAN LIFE

The main work of the Holy Spirit is in the life of the believer. The Holy Spirit is a primary cause of one's regeneration and sanctification.

The New Testament uses a few important terms to describe the work of the Holy Spirit in the life of a believer.

Baptism in the Spirit

When John the Baptist began his ministry, he said that one would come after him who would baptize with the Holy Spirit (Mt 3:11; Mk 1:8; Lk 3:16; Jn 1:33). Right before his ascension, Jesus said that in a few days the disciples would be baptized with the Holy Spirit (Acts 1:5). This occurred at Pentecost. After that Cornelius was baptized by the Holy Spirit (Acts 11:16).

So what is baptism in the Holy Spirit? There are two different views on this: the Pentecostal view and the classical view.[1]

The Pentecostal view says that the Christian life has two stages. First, a person is converted through faith in Jesus. Then, at a later point in life, the believer is baptized by or in the Holy Spirit. The usual

---

[1]See W. Grudem, *Systematic Theology*, pp. 763-84.

evidence of the baptism in the Holy Spirit is the speaking in tongues. Sometimes this second stage is called a second blessing or being filled with the Holy Spirit.

Traditional Pentecostalists find support for their position in the day of Pentecost (Acts 2), the Samaritan conversion (Acts 8), the conversion of Saul (Acts 9), the conversion of Cornelius (Acts 10) and the conversion experience at Ephesus (Acts 19).

But it is not clear that each of these conversions was a two-stage experience. Since the Christian church began at Pentecost, the outpouring of the Spirit on that day was not really a second blessing. The disciples at Ephesus (Acts 19) had only received John's baptism and not a Christian baptism, so their experience was not really a two-stage experience. Paul's conversion was certainly a one-stage experience. But was the Samaritan experience (Acts 8) the normal pattern or an exception?

The second view is the classical view. This view of the baptism in the Spirit is that the baptism of the Spirit occurs at conversion. This view finds support from 1 Corinthians 12:13, where Paul tells the imperfect church at Corinth that "we were all baptized by one Spirit into one body." Every member of that imperfect church was baptized in the Holy Spirit.

Michael Green says: "the baptism in the Spirit is an initiatory experience. The Spirit of God brings people into the family of God."[2] The Holy Spirit is active at the beginning of the Christian experience during the time of conversion.

---

[2]M. Green, *I Believe in the Holy Spirit* (London: Hodder and Stoughton, 1985), p. 173.

Fullness of the Spirit

The life of a Christian should be dominated by the Holy Spirit. The New Testament speaks of persons being full of the Spirit and being filled with the Spirit.

A few times the New Testament speaks of a person or persons being full of the Spirit. Jesus himself was "full of the Holy Spirit," according to Luke (4:1). In the book of Acts, the Twelve chose seven men to assist them. These Seven were "full of the Spirit and wisdom" (Acts 6:3). One of the Seven was Stephen, "a man full of faith and of the Holy Spirit" (Acts 6:5; cf. 7:55). Barnabas was "a good man, full of the Holy Spirit and faith" (Acts 11:24).

To be full of the Spirit is a general description of a Spirit-filled believer. Such a person "is habitually governed and controlled by the Lord the Spirit, just as Jesus was."[3] This is a continuous state for some believers.

But sometimes at critical points in one's ministry, a person has a sudden filling of the Spirit with various results. On the day of Pentecost the disciples were filled with the Spirit and spoke in tongues (Acts 2:4). Some days later Peter was filled with the Spirit and spoke boldly (Acts 4:8). Soon after that the disciples were filled with the Spirit and spoke boldly (Acts 4:31). Twice we read that Paul was filled with the Spirit, and once he spoke boldly (Acts 9:17; 13:9).

We discover from the above that being filled with the Spirit does not necessarily result in the speaking in tongues. Rather, the Spirit empowers believers to act in powerful ways depending on the circumstances.

The Christian life is a Spirit-filled life. Sanctification is a life-long process. So Paul urges every believer to "be filled with the Spirit" (Eph

---

[3]M. Green, *I Believe in the Holy Spirit*, p. 180.

5:18). Every Christian should try to live a life that is dominated by the Holy Spirit. Every Christian should seek to be full of the Holy Spirit.

The gifts and fruit of the Spirit

Every Christian will have some special gifts from the Holy Spirit. The spiritual gifts in Greek are called *charismata* (e.g., Rom 12:6) or *pneumatika* (e.g., 1 Cor 14:1).

There are different lists of the gifts: Romans 12:6-8; 1 Corinthians 12:8-10, 28, 29-30; Ephesians 4:11; 1 Peter 4:10-11. The gifts include prophecy, serving, teaching, encouraging, giving, leadership, showing mercy, speaking in tongues and interpreting tongues.

A few things are clear about the spiritual gifts. First, not every person will have all of the gifts. Second, not all of the gifts are "supernatural." Some of the gifts are rather ordinary like teaching, giving and showing mercy. Third, there is no suggestion that speaking in tongues, for example, is more important than the other gifts. Often speaking in tongues occurs towards the bottom of the list.

In addition, one must remember the purpose of the gifts. Paul says that Jesus gave these spiritual gifts "to prepare God's people for works of service, so that the body of Christ may be built up" (Eph 4:12). The purpose of the gifts is the building up of the church, not self-glorification. Every believer should try to know what one's own gifts are so that one's local church may be built up.

But while a believer may have only a few spiritual gifts, every believer should have all of the fruit of the Spirit. Paul lists nine fruits: "love, joy, peace, patience, kindness, goodness, faithfulness, gentleness and self-control" (Gal 5:22-23).

If a person is truly filled with the Holy Spirit, that person will have a full measure of all of the fruit of the Spirit.

Study Questions

1.   What do you think baptism in the Holy Spirit is?
2.   What is the fullness of the Spirit?
3.   When and why is a person filled with the Spirit?
4.   What is the fruit of the Spirit?
5.   What are the most important gifts of the Spirit? Are some gifts more important than others?
6.   **Essay:** Write an essay on the gifts of the Spirit.

CHAPTER 20

THE NATURE OF THE CHURCH

Christians should not exist in isolation; rather, they should live in community. The community of Christians is called the church.

The New Testament speaks frequently of the church. The Greek word for church is *ekklēsia*. Strictly speaking, an *ekklēsia* is an assembly of people. In Ephesus, for example, an *ekklēsia* or assembly or mob of people loudly protested against Paul and for three hours shouted, "Great is Diana of the Ephesians" (Acts 19:32,41). But the city clerk called for discussion in a legal *ekklēsia* (Acts 19:39).

Usually, however, in the New Testament the *ekklēsia* is the assembly or community belonging to God or Christ. This we commonly call the church.

The church can be defined as "the new people of God"[1] or "the community of believers."[2]

Images of the church

The Bible uses different metaphors or pictures to describe the church.[3]

---

[1] G.E. Ladd, *A Theology of the New Testament* (Grand Rapids: Eerdmans, 1974), p. 537.

[2] L. Berkhof, *Systematic Theology* (Grand Rapids: Eerdmans, 1939), p. 571.

[3] See B. Milne, *Know the Truth*, pp. 210-14; Paul Minear, *Images of the Church in the New Testament* (Philadelphia: Wesminster, 1960).

Sometimes the church is seen as the *people of God*. Peter calls the Christians in Asia Minor "a chosen people" (1 Pet 2:9). This image suggests that the church is the new Israel.

The church is also the *body of Christ*. Paul in his letter to Corinth compares a body with many parts to the church with many spiritual gifts. He concludes: "Now you are the body of Christ" (1 Cor 12:27). This image tells us of the unity and diversity of the church.

The church is also the *temple of God*. Peter tells the Christians that they "like living stones, are being built into a spiritual house" (1 Pet 2:5). Paul says: "you yourselves are God's temple" (1 Cor 3:16). The church, like the Old Testament temple, should be holy.

The church is also the *bride of Christ* (see Eph 5:25-32; Rev 21:2). This image expresses the love and union that exists between Jesus and his church.

The church is *the family of God*. Christians are "members of God's household" (Eph 2:19; cf. 1 Tim 3:15). This reminds us of the fact that we are adopted as sons and daughters of God (see Rom 8:16-17).

The church is the *flock* of Jesus. Jesus is "the good shepherd" who "lays down his life for the sheep" (Jn 10:11; cf. vs. 14). We are reminded that Jesus loves us and cares for us.

The church is also part of the *vine*. Jesus said, "I am the vine; you are the branches" (Jn 15:5). This image speaks of the union between Christ and the believer. In order to bear fruit, we must abide in Christ, and he in us.

The attributes of the church

The above images and the creeds of the church suggest four attributes. The *Nicene Creed* says: "We believe in one, holy, catholic (universal) and apostolic church." (See similar wording in the *Apostles' Creed*.)

First, the church is *one*. Even though we have hundreds of denominations, yet the church is one in its beliefs and in its union with Christ. The images of the body and the temple emphasize this oneness. Paul writes: "There is one body and one Spirit . . . one Lord, one faith, one baptism [and] one God and Father of all" (Eph 4:4-6).

Second, the church is *holy*. The church is holy in two ways: through faith in Christ we are justified or declared holy before God's court of law; but we are also sanctified or made holy in our Christian lives.

Third, the church is *catholic* or *universal*. In other words, the church is found in all parts of the world. The church is drawn from every tribe and nation.

Finally, the church is *apostolic*. This means that the church is built on the teaching of the twelve apostles. Jesus said to Peter that "on this rock I will build my church" (Mt 16:18). Paul said that the church is "built on the foundation of the apostles and prophets" (Eph 2:20). The apostles were those who were closest to Jesus. Much of the New Testament was written by the apostles. Our theology should therefore be apostolic.

Visible and invisible church

The church, of course, is visible to the human eye. The visible church is the church that we see meeting every Sunday.

The Anglican *Thirty-Nine Articles* defines the visible church as "a congregation of faithful men and women in which the pure Word of God is preached and the Sacraments be duly ministered according to Christ's ordinance."[4]

The visible church is an institute (institution) with officers and public worship services and usually—but not always—a church

---

[4]"The Thirty-Nine Articles of Religion," in *The Book of Common Prayer* (Abuja, 2007), p. 503.

building. The visible church is, for example, the Roman Catholic, Anglican, Lutheran, Presbyterian, Pentecostal or African churches among us.

But the problem that we discover is that there are unbelievers or nominal Christians ("church-goers") in our visible churches. This was also the case during the Middle Ages and Reformation. Then the Roman Catholic hierarchy was particularly corrupt.

So John Wycliffe and John Hus said that the church is the true believers of all times and not the Roman Catholic Church hierarchy. For them the true church is the invisible church, not the visible one.

John Calvin distinguished between the visible church and the invisible church. The invisible church is all the true believers, visible only to God; the visible church is the church that we humans see with our eyes.[5]

John Wesley defined "the catholic or universal Church" as "all the persons in the universe whom God has so called out of the world." But this universal (or invisible) church manifests itself in particular (visible) churches.[6]

In the end, the church is one. We should think of two concentric circles: the bigger circle is the visible church comprising the true believers and also the hypocrites; the smaller circle is the true believers or the invisible church.

The marks of the church

It is regrettable that in history the church has often become unfaithful. So theologians have identified marks to determine whether a church is essentially true or false.

---

[5]J. Calvin, *The Institutes of the Christian Religion*, 4.1.7 (pp. 1021-22).
[6]J.Wesley, "On the Church," in *The Works of John Wesley* 6:395-96.

John Calvin said that the "distinguishing marks of the church" are "the preaching of the Word and the [correct] observance of the sacraments."[7] The Anglican *Thirty-Nine Articles* speaks of a visible church where "the pure Word of God is preached and the Sacraments be duly ministered."[8]

Scripture as the Word of God is a central test of how true or false a church might be. This is particularly relevant today. There are Prosperity Churches which have distorted the Word of God. Are they then true or false churches?

John Wesley said: "those congregations in which the pure word of God ... is not preached are no parts either of the Church of England, or the Church catholic."[9] But he went on to emphasize holiness as an essential part of the church.

Other marks may also define the church. One pastor suggests six marks of a true church: joy, holiness, truth, mission, unity and love.[10] If these marks are absent, a true church is certainly not present.

A true church is one that will conform to the ideal in Scripture. A true church will have true doctrine and a godly lifestyle. The idea of a true church is an ideal that every church should strive to attain to.

---

[7] J. Calvin, *Institutes of the Christian Religion*, 4.1.10 (p. 1024).

[8] "The Thirty-Nine Articles of Religion," p. 503.

[9] J. Wesley, "On the Church," pp. 397 ff.

[10] J. Boice, *Foundations of the Christian Faith* (Downers Grove: InterVarsity Press, 1986), pp. 576-85.

Study Questions

1. How would you define the church?
2. Define the relation between visible and the invisible church. Are they one church or two churches?
3. Which images of the church teach holiness?
4. What are the four attributes of the church?
5. What do you think are the marks of a true church?
6. **Essay:** Write an essay on whether Prosperity Churches are true churches or false churches.

CHAPTER 21

THE LIFE OF THE CHURCH

The church in its visible form is an organization or institution. So what is the government of this institution? How does it function in this world?

Church officers

The chief officer of the church is Jesus Christ. Jesus is the head and the king of the church. Every human officer operates under the rule of Jesus Christ.

During and after Pentecost, there were extraordinary and ordinary officers. The special or extraordinary officers were the apostles and prophets; the ordinary officers were the elders (or overseers) and deacons.[1]

The first office is that of apostle. An apostle (*apostolos*) is one who is sent. In a general sense, every Christian is an apostle or messenger. But in a narrow sense, an apostle is one who had seen Jesus after his resurrection and who was commissioned by Jesus as an apostle.

At the beginning of his ministry Jesus chose twelve disciples or apostles (Lk 6:13). These disciples were close to Jesus during his entire

---

[1]See L. Berkhof, *Systematic Theology*, pp. 585-87; W. Grudem, *Systematic Theology*, pp. 905-20.

ministry. After Judas betrayed Jesus, the eleven other disciples chose one who was "a witness with us of [Christ's] resurrection." According to their prayer, he was chosen by Jesus. So Matthias "was added to the eleven apostles" (Acts 1:21-26).

Paul was also an apostle. He wrote, "Am I not an apostle? Have I not seen Jesus our Lord?" (1 Cor 9:1; 15:9). Barnabas and James were also apostles (Acts 14:14; Gal 1:19).

But if an apostle is one who has seen Jesus, then the office of apostle in the narrow sense no longer exists today.

A prophet is one who speaks for God. In a general sense, every Christian is a prophet when he or she speaks the word of God. But in a narrow sense, a prophet is one who receives special revelations from God. The book of Acts tells us of the prophets Agabus (11:28), Judas and Silas (15:32), and other prophets in Antioch (13:1).

The office of prophet today is not a regular office in the church. But there may be people in our churches today who have special revelations from God or the gift of prophecy. However their "prophecies" need to be tested by the church.

The first ordinary or regular office is that of elder or overseer. The Greek word for elder is *presbuteros*; the Greek word for bishop or overseer is *episkopos*.

On his way to Jerusalem, Paul met with the elders (*presbuteroi*) of Ephesus (Acts 20:17). In his speech to them, he called them overseers (*episkopoi*) (Acts 20:28). We conclude that elders and overseers are two names for the same office.

(The King James Version translates *episkopos* as "bishop." But the bishop is a later development in the church. The NIV "overseer" is a better translation.)

The early local churches were governed by elders. The plural elders were "the main governing group in New Testament churches."[2]

When Paul and Barnabas established churches, they appointed elders for each church (Acts 14:23). Peter instructed the elders of the churches to be faithful shepherds and overseers (1 Pet 5:1-2). James presupposes the elders as the rulers of the local church (Jas 5:14).

Paul in 1 Timothy 5:17 distinguishes between ruling elders and teaching elders. The elders "direct the affairs of the church"; but some elders have the task of "preaching and teaching." The teaching elders would be our pastors today.

The early church also had deacons. The Greek word *diakonos* suggests one who ministers or serves. The church at Philippi had two offices: that of overseer and deacon (Phil 1:1). Paul wrote to Timothy about both overseers and deacons (1 Tim 3:1-13).

But we really don't know the job description of a deacon. Some church traditions think that the deacon is to minister to the physical needs of the community, as the "Seven" in Acts 6 did. But other traditions think that the deacon assists the pastor.

Our churches today have grown beyond the size of the small early church. Therefore today we have offices that are not found in the New Testament like President, General Secretary and Bishop.

The functions of a church

So why does the church exist? What is the purpose or the functions of a church? Scholars suggest at least four functions or purposes.[3]

---

[2]W. Grudem, *Systematic Theology*, p. 912; see M. Erickson, *Christian Theology*, pp. 1052-59.

[3]See M. Erickson, *Christian Theology*, pp. 1052-59; W. Grudem, *Systematic Theology*, pp. 867-69.

The first function of the church is *worship*. Paul tells the Corinthian Christians to come together on the first day of the week (1 Cor 16:2). He also expects that the Colossian church will "sing psalms, hymns and spiritual songs with gratitude in [their] hearts to God" (Col 3:16). The book of Psalms has many hymns of praise which were used by Israel in the Old Testament times. The Christian church too will want to praise God in a similar way.

The second function of the church is *edification*. The church receives many spiritual gifts "to prepare God's people for works of service so that the body of Christ might be built up" (Eph 4:12). Teaching and preaching are central tasks of the church. Edification includes pastoral care. But pastoral care can be done both by the pastor and elders and by the members. Paul tells the Ephesians to bear one another's burdens (Eph 4:2). The church is like a body where each member cares for each other. "God has combined the members of the body . . . so that . . . its parts should have equal concern for each other" (1 Cor 12:24-25).

Evangelism is a third function of the church. The church is "the salt of the earth" and "the light of the world." It is "a city on a hill" (Mt 5:13-14). The church has the task to "go and make disciples of all nations" (Mt 28:19). Evangelism and missions are a central task of the church.

Social concern is another function. There are many poor among us. There is injustice in our society. The church should show the compassion of Jesus to the poor in our society, and especially in the church. The church should also take a prophetic stance against the injustice in our world.

Church and Kingdom

The church is a visible manifestation of the kingdom of God. The church consists of people who have submitted to the reign of Jesus Christ. The kingdom of God should be seen in the church.

Some traditions have thus concluded that the church and the kingdom of God are identical. But a comprehensive view of the kingdom of God suggests that the kingdom is bigger and broader than the church.

In actuality, it is the kingdom or rule of God that creates the church. The church then witnesses to the kingdom of God.[4]

The Gospels tell us of Jesus who sent out the twelve disciples (the church) to preach the kingdom of heaven and to heal the sick, raise the dead, cleanse the lepers and drive out the demons (Matt 10:5-8; Lk 9:1-2). The kingdom of God here is the transforming rule of Christ in all of society. The church as an institute and as the people of God is God's instrument in bringing about the kingdom of God in its full sense.

From the pulpit, the church should preach the kingdom of God. Inside and outside the visible institutional church, members should bring to realization the kingdom of God. When the church as an institute or as individual members preaches and practices justice and shows mercy, the kingdom of God becomes a reality. When the church preaches salvation in Jesus Christ, the kingdom of God then comes about.

"In summary, while there is an inseparable relationship between the Kingdom and the church, they are not to be identified. The Kingdom takes its point of departure from God, the church from

---

[4]See G.E. Ladd, *A Theology of the New Testament*, pp. 111-15.

humans."[5] The church as an institute is just one aspect of life; the kingdom of God is found in every part of life.

Study Questions

1.   What are the broad and narrow definitions of apostle?
2.   What are the duties of an elder or an overseer?
3.   What do you think is the role of a deacon?
4.   What are four functions of the church?
5.   Are the church and the kingdom of God identical? Explain.
6.   **Essay:** Write an essay on the ideal elder. (Consider 1 Timothy 2 and Titus 1.)

---

[5]G.E. Ladd, *A Theology of the New Testament*, p. 119.

CHAPTER 22

~~~~~~

THE SACRAMENTS

Before Jesus ascended into heaven he instituted two ordinances: baptism and the Lord's Supper. Sometimes these ordinances are called sacraments. Sacraments give visible expression to our faith. They are visible signs or pictures of the salvation that we have in Jesus.

The Christian church has wrestled with the question of the sacraments. This chapter looks at the history and the theology of the sacraments.[1]

History of the idea of the sacraments

The Latin word *sacramentum* was applied to the church ordinances by the early North African church. Originally, a *sacramentum* was an oath or a mystery. St. Augustine, from North Africa, said that a sacrament is a sign and a spiritual reality. He said that a sacrament is a visible sign of an invisible grace.

The medieval Roman Catholic Church concluded that there are seven sacraments: baptism, confirmation, eucharist, marriage, penance, unction (anointing) and ordination. All of these sacraments are means of grace. In other words, they convey grace. But is this grace

---

[1]See A. McGrath, *Christian Theology* (Oxford: Blackwell, 1997), pp. 494-520, for a historical discussion of the sacraments.

conveyed automatically or not? The Catholic Church tended to say that the grace is given automatically, even if faith is not always present.

But Martin Luther objected. He said that faith is essential in the Lord's Supper for grace to be received. For him a sacrament is a promise and a sign. Faith needs to receive and accept the promise of the sacrament.

Luther thought that there are only two sacraments: baptism and the Lord's Supper. He thought that the other Catholic sacraments are not really sacraments since they lack a sign. Yet Luther agreed with the Catholics that the sacraments are a means of grace.

The Anglican Church follows both St. Augustine and Martin Luther. The Anglican Catechism defines the sacraments as "the outward and visible signs of inward and spiritual grace."[2] The water of baptism and the bread and wine of the Lord's Supper are signs of the grace that is given through the sacrament.

John Calvin agreed. For him a sacrament is a sign and a seal of our salvation.

But Ulrich Zwingli and the Anabaptists disagreed with Luther, the Anglicans and Calvin. Zwingli and the Anabaptists thought that the sacraments are only signs or pictures of our salvation. The Baptist tradition generally thinks that the sacraments are mainly symbolic.

For this reason, many in the Baptist and the free church tradition use the term "church ordinance" instead of "sacrament." (It should be noted that the Church of the Brethren [Ekklesiyar Yan'uwa a Nigeria] observes three church ordinances: baptism, Lord's Supper and foot washing.)

In most of the above positions, the sacraments are pictures of our salvation in Jesus Christ. But Prosperity Theology has changed the sacraments from a means of grace to a means of prosperity. Prosperity

---

[2]"The Catechism," in *The Book of Common Prayer* (Abuja, 2007), p. 492.

Theology also teaches that health and power are received automatically from the sacrament.

David Oyedepo, for example, calls the Lord's Supper a "miracle meal." He believes that the bread and wine give "supernatural strength." He claims that all bodily sicknesses "will be neutralized by eating the flesh of Jesus." All illnesses "will be swallowed up in victory by the meal of life."

Oyedepo also seems to add another sacrament, namely, anointing. He says that anointing brings "sustenance, performance, success, breakthrough and fulfillment."[3] Again, for Oyedepo anointing oil seems to work automatically. But the focus of the "sacrament" is then changed from spiritual salvation to physical health and well-being. Also, in Prosperity Theology baptism seems to be less important.

Theology of the sacraments

There is a wide diversity of theology and practice in respect to the sacraments. Yet most Christian theologians agree on a few basic things.

First, a sacrament is a visible sign of a spiritual reality. Baptism and the Lord's Supper are pictures of the salvation that we have in Jesus. Baptism pictures our dying and rising with Christ and the washing away of our sins. The Lord's Supper pictures the salvation we have through the death of Jesus.

Second, our faith is strengthened by the sacraments. We are reminded of the work of Christ on the cross that brings salvation to those who believe. In some sense, grace is conveyed through the sacraments.

Third, one must guard against perversions of the sacraments. Jesus said that the cup is "my blood of the covenant, which is poured out

---

[3]D. Oyedepo, *Anointing for Breakthrough* (Lagos: Dominion, 2002), p. 63; quoted by Asamoah-Gyadu, *Contemporary Pentecostal Theology*, pp. 134-35.

for many for the forgiveness of sins" (Mt 26:28). Jesus also says that "whoever eats my flesh and drinks my blood has eternal life" (Jn 6:53). The Lord's Supper is a sign of the forgiveness of sins and the eternal life that we receive through the death of Jesus Christ. It is not a magic potion to ward off sickness or to guarantee health and wealth. The sacraments represent the salvation that we have in Jesus.

Study Questions

1. Define a sacrament.
2. In light of your definition, is penance a sacrament?
3. Describe the promise offered in baptism and the Lord's Supper.
4. To what extent are the sacraments (or church ordinances) means of grace?
5. **Essay:** Write an essay on the use of sacraments in the Prosperity Theology churches.

CHAPTER 23

BAPTISM

The first sacrament or church ordinance is Christian baptism. Water baptism is a rite of initiation into the Christian church.

Christian baptism was instituted by Jesus after his resurrection. Jesus then said, "Go and make disciples of all nations, baptizing them in the name of the Father and of the Son and of the Holy Spirit" (Mt 28:19). Soon after that on the day of Pentecost, Peter invited the new believers to "repent and be baptized . . . in the name of Jesus Christ for the forgiveness of your sins" (Acts 2:38). Three thousand people were then baptized.

Christian baptism should be distinguished from John's baptism. John's baptism was a preparation for the coming of the Messiah and the kingdom of God. It was not a baptism in the name of the Father, Son and Holy Spirit. John's baptism was a messianic and pre-Christian baptism. Christian baptism began at Pentecost.

The sacrament of (water) baptism should also be distinguished from Holy Spirit baptism. Holy Spirit baptism occurs when the Spirit comes upon a person, either causing faith or causing a second blessing. Water baptism is a visible symbol of an invisible reality, and is thus different from Spirit baptism.

Theology of baptism

The verb "to baptize" comes from the Greek word meaning "to dip" or "to immerse." Baptism then is a ritual washing.

The use of water in baptism is important. Water is often used for cleansing or purification. The water in baptism can thus signify the washing away of our sins. Peter invited the people to be baptized for the forgiveness of their sins (Acts 2:38). Paul alludes to baptism when he calls it "the washing of rebirth" (Titus 3:5).

But waters in the Old Testament are often a sign of death. The waters of the Red Sea were threatening to the Israelites and Pharaoh; the waters around Jonah were a threat to Jonah's life.

So Paul says that baptism is union with Christ in his death and burial. He says that "all of us who were baptized in Christ Jesus were baptized into his death. We were therefore buried with him through baptism into death" (Rom 6:3-4).

Baptism is therefore participation in the death and also the resurrection of Jesus. Through the death of Jesus we have the forgiveness of sins. Through his resurrection we have new life.

In the deepest sense, baptism represents union with Christ and his body, the church. Christians have been baptized "into Christ" (Rom 6:3; Gal 3:27).

Baptism is a rite of initiation into the church, which is the body of Christ. Through baptism we become members of the church of Christ. But baptism also represents the spiritual union of a believer with Jesus Christ. Through baptism we become one with Jesus Christ and his church.

John Calvin says: "Baptism is the sign of the initiation by which we are received into the society of the church, in order that, engrafted in

Christ, we may be reckoned among God's children."[1] Through baptism we are engrafted into Jesus Christ and we become children of God.

Infant or believer's baptism?

Christians are generally agreed on the above. But they disagree as to the subjects of baptism. Who are to be baptized—adults or infants?

The Baptist position says that only those who are old enough to understand and believe may be baptized. Baptists assume that infants are unable to believe. Therefore only believers who are of age may be baptized.

Baptists believe that faith must necessarily precede baptism. The longer ending of Mark records the words of Jesus: "Whoever believes and is baptized will be saved" (Mk 16:16).

In the book of Acts, faith generally preceded baptism. On the day of Pentecost the people believed and were baptized (Acts 2:41). Cornelius believed and was baptized (Acts 10:47-48). Lydia and the Philippian jailor believed and were baptized (Acts 16:14-15, 31-33), as were others. But of course these baptisms occurred in a first-generation, missionary setting.

Other theologians think that children and even infants may have been included in these baptisms. We read that the "household" (*oikos*) of Cornelius, Lydia and the Philippian jailor were also baptized (Acts 11:14; 16:15,31). Of course, no one knows who were in these households. Perhaps children and infants were included; perhaps servants and older members of the family were included.

Those who advocate infant baptism go back to the Old Testament. They assume a parallelism between male circumcision and Christian baptism. In Genesis 17, male circumcision was the rite of initiation into the covenant with God, and baby boys were circumcised. In the

---

[1] J. Calvin, *Institutes of the Christian Religion*, 4.15.1 (p. 1303).

New Testament, baptism is the rite of initiation into the new covenant between God and his people, and, it is assumed, infant children of believers should be baptized.

Those who advocate infant baptism believe that God claims these children as his own. They believe that the promise of grace comes first, and the faith should come later.

Christians will disagree on aspects of baptism. But we all agree that baptism is a sign of our union with Christ and his church. Baptism is a sign that we belong to Jesus. It is a sign—and perhaps a seal—that we have died and raised with Christ. It is a sign that we have come out of the world and that we belong to Jesus.

Study Questions

1.   What does the water of baptism symbolize?
2.   What is the relation between water baptism and Holy Spirit baptism?
3.   Is the baptism of John the Baptist a Christian baptism? Explain.
4.   What is the significance of Christian baptism?
5.   **Essay:** Write an essay defending either infant baptism or believer's baptism.

CHAPTER 24

THE LORD'S SUPPER

The second sacrament or church ordinance is the Lord's Supper or the Eucharist. This sacrament was instituted by Christ. Just before his death Jesus shared the bread and wine with his disciples and then said: "do this in remembrance of me" (1 Cor 11:24-25).

The Lord's Supper is a sacrament because it is a visible sign of an invisible grace. The broken bread and shed wine are pictures of the crucified body of Jesus and the salvation we have through the death of Jesus.

Interpretations of the Lord's Supper

The church in the last two thousand years has reflected on the meaning of the Lord's Supper. Different views have emerged.

The Roman Catholic Church in the Middle Ages developed the doctrine of *transubstantiation*. This is the belief that the bread and wine of the Eucharist are changed into the body and blood of Jesus. Thus the Roman Catholics believe that a believer actually eats the body and blood of Jesus. Christ's body is then sacrificed every time the Eucharist is celebrated.

Martin Luther rejected *transubstantiation* and taught consubstantiation. For him the body of Christ is present every time the

Lord's Supper is celebrated. The bread is not the body of Christ but the body of Christ is present above and under and alongside of the bread. Luther felt strongly about the real presence of the body of Christ at the Lord's Supper.

In his *The Babylonian Captivity of the Church*, Luther said that the Lord's Supper is "a promise of the forgiveness of sins made to us by God." If then the Lord's Supper is a promise, "then access to it is to be gained, not with any works, or powers, or merits of one's own, but by faith alone."[1] Faith is essential for receiving the Lord's Supper.

Ulrich Zwingli and John Calvin agreed that faith is essential in partaking in the Lord's Supper. But they felt that it is logically impossible for the body of Christ to be omnipresent. They said that Christ's body is localized in heaven and only his divinity is present at the Lord's Supper.

Despite its differences, historic Christianity has agreed that the Lord's Supper is a Christian ritual that signifies the forgiveness of sins through the sacrifice of Christ. Thus to say that the Lord's Supper is a "miracle meal" is a complete perversion of the sacrament. The Lord's Supper is not a magic guarantee of prosperity, but it is a reminder that our sins are forgiven through the death and resurrection of Jesus. The focus of the Lord's Supper is not prosperity or protection but the forgiveness of sins.

Theology of the Lord's Supper

So what are the theology and the significance of the Lord's Supper? A key text is found in Paul's first letter to the Corinthians, where he says that the cup is "participation (*koinōnia*) in the blood of Christ" and the bread is "participation in the body of Christ" (1 Cor 10:16).

---

[1]M. Luther, "The Babylonian Captivity of the Church," in *Luther's Works* 36:38-39.

When a person eats or drinks of the Lord's Supper, that person is participating in the crucifixion of Jesus. He or she is benefiting from the completed work of Jesus on the cross. He or she is receiving the "blood of the covenant, which is poured out for many for the forgiveness of sins" (Mt 26:28).

The Lord's Supper also symbolizes the unity of the church since believers are now in fellowship (*koinōnia*) with each other. The sacrament of the Lord's Supper in the early church of Corinth was a proclamation of unity in a divided church.

The Lord's Supper also affirms our fellowship and union with God himself. John Calvin said that baptism is a sign of our being engrafted in Christ; and the Lord's Supper is "a help whereby we may be engrafted into Christ's body, or, engrafted, may grow more and more together with him, until he perfectly joins us with him in the heavenly life."[2] Feeding on the body of Christ is a symbol of our oneness with Christ.

Baptism and the Lord's Supper are both visible signs of our salvation. They are both signs—and perhaps seals—of our oneness with God and with Jesus Christ. They are therefore central to the life of the church.

---

[2]J. Calvin, *Institutes of the Christian Religion*, 4.17.33 (pp. 1407-1408).

Study Questions

1. What is the Roman Catholic doctrine of transubstantiation?
2. Compare Luther's and Zwingli's view of the presence of the body of Christ at the Lord's Supper.
3. Distinguish Zwingli's and Calvin's view of the Lord's Supper.
4. Explain how union with Christ is central to the doctrine of salvation and the sacraments.
5. **Essay:** Write an essay on your personal view of the presence of Christ in the Lord's Supper.

CHAPTER 25

THE KINGDOM OF GOD

The kingdom of God is an eschatological concept. The Old Testament person expected that in the future at the end of time the kingdom of God would come. Then the Messiah would reign with peace and prosperity.

But when Jesus came, he proclaimed that the kingdom of God was already at hand. The eschatological kingdom of God was already present, but it was not yet fully present. This is the "already-not yet" dimension to the kingdom of God.

The present kingdom of God

The kingdom of God is already present now. Jesus is the King of the kingdom.

When Jesus rose from the dead, he received authority to reign. He said, "All authority in heaven and on earth has been given to me" (Mt 28:18).

Then Jesus ascended into heaven and sat at the right hand of God the Father. God "raised him from the dead and seated him at his right hand in the heavenly realms . . . . And God placed all things under his feet" (Eph 1:20-22).

The reign of Jesus is from his ascension until the end of time. Paul says, "He must reign until he has put all his enemies under his feet." Then, "the end will come when he hands over the kingdom to God the Father after he has destroyed all dominion, authority and power" (1 Cor 15:25,24).

Jesus is reigning now. But Satan also has power. Satan is called "the god of this age" (2 Cor 4:4). So there is warfare between the kingdom of God and the kingdom of Satan. "Our struggle is not against flesh and blood, but against the rulers, the authorities, the powers of this dark world and the spiritual forces of evil in the heavenly realms" (Eph. 6:12).

The kingdom of God includes all of life: family, school, work, government, the environment and the institutional church. But the kingdom of Satan is also found in all of life—including the institutional church. (When church leaders or members do not obey Christ, the kingdom of Satan is present.)

The kingdom of God in its redemptive sense is the rule of God through Jesus Christ in all of creation. The kingdom of God is present wherever and whenever a person obeys God. The kingdom of Satan is present wherever and whenever a person disobeys God.

So Jesus is reigning now, at the right hand of God the Father.

The millennium

The book of Revelation in its unique way describes a thousand-year reign of Christ. This is called the millennium. In Revelation 20, John saw a vision of Satan being bound for a thousand years while Christ reigned for the same thousand years. After the thousand years, Satan will be released for a final battle, and then the Last Judgment would take place.

So when is the thousand-year reign of Christ? What is this millennium? There are at least three answers to this question.

1. Pre-millennialism

Pre-millennialism is the view that the return of Christ will be before ("pre") the millennium. This view believes that Jesus will secretly rapture the believers, bind Satan and then set up a physical thousand-year reign in earthly Jerusalem. This will be a reign of peace and prosperity. At the end of this reign, Satan will be released and there will be a final battle. Satan will be finally defeated, there will be a Last Judgment and the eternal kingdom of God will begin.

This view is popular in some circles. It presupposes a literal reading of Old Testament prophecies and the book of Revelation. But how literally should one read prophecy and Revelation? Should one not read prophecy and apocalyptic literature more symbolically? Also, is Christ reigning from heaven or in the physical Jerusalem?

2. Post-millennialism

Post-millennialism believes that the return of Christ will be after ("post") the millennium. For them the millennium will not be a literal thousand-year reign on earth. Instead our present age will gradually become the glorious reign of Jesus. As the Gospel spreads globally, the world will become increasingly better. Justice and righteousness will flourish throughout the world with the result of peace and prosperity. Evil will be greatly reduced. Jesus will reign from heaven for a long period of time before his final return.

This is an optimistic view of world history that was developed in the 18th, 19th and early 20th centuries when the world seemed to be getting better. Unfortunately, today's world seems to be getting worse. Our world does not seem to be moving in a post-millennial direction.

3. Realized millennialism (a-millennialism)

The a-millennial position teaches that there is no ("a"=no) literal millennium. This position is also called the realized millennial view since it thinks that the millennium is present now. This view believes that the thousand years of Revelation is actually the very long period of time between the first and second comings of Jesus.

Realized millennialism believes that Satan was defeated at the first coming of Jesus. (See John 12:31: "Now the prince of this world will be driven out.") When Jesus paid for our sins on the cross, Satan lost his power. This view has a symbolic interpretation of the binding of Satan and the thousand years. (Satan is bound on a very long chain.) Despite the evil in this world, Jesus is still reigning at the right hand of the Father.

Some people will object to this view since Satan's power is still very great in this world. Others are looking for an ideal millennial kingdom on this earth. But the realized millennial view believes that Jesus is already ruling through the lives of churches and Christians throughout the world.

Christians will have different views on the question of millennium. But we all believe that the reign of Christ is both present and future. We all believe that Satan will be defeated in the end. And we all wait eagerly for the second coming of Jesus.

Study Questions

1. Describe the reign of Christ according to 1 Corinthians 15:24-28.
2. Describe the kingdom of God in Nigeria today.
3. Why is post-millennialism not a viable option today?
4. Compare and contrast pre-millennialism and realized millennialism.
5. **Essay:** Write an essay on your view of the millennium of Revelation 20.

CHAPTER 26

SIGNS OF THE END

Once the disciples asked Jesus what would be the sign of his coming and the end of the age (Mt 24:3). Jesus responded by saying that there would be many eschatological signs.

Yet we are already in the eschatological time. The eschatological kingdom of God is already present. So the signs of the end are both present and future.

Particular signs

Jesus lists various signs of the end in the Olivet Discourse (found in Matthew 24, Mark 13 and Luke 21). There are three categories of these signs.[1]

Some signs are evidence of God's grace. Jesus said that the Gospel must be preached in the whole world as a testimony to all tribes or nations before the end will come (Mt 24:14; Mk 13:10). Paul suggests a conversion of the Jews before the end (Rom 11:26). The delay in Christ's return is grace for the Gentiles and the Jews who are yet to believe.

Other signs are an indication of God's judgment. There will be wars, famines and earthquakes before the return of Christ (Mt 24:6-7).

---

[1]See A. Hoekema, *The Bible and the Future* (Grand Rapids: Eerdmans, 1979), pp. 137-63.

Of course, these signs are not just future: the world has experienced them from the beginning. But they are a reminder of the effects of sin in this world. They are also called "the beginning of birth pains" (Mt 24:8), suggesting the anticipation of the future joy of Christ's return.

The third category of signs is those things that stand in opposition to God and his kingdom. In particular, the end times will see tribulation, apostasy and the antichrist figure. Jesus speaks of false prophets, persecution, apostasy and "the abomination that causes desolation" (Mt 24:9-15).

Of course the church has experienced these things throughout its history, but it seems that there will be an intensification of such persecution in the last days.

The antichrist is one of the signs of the end. Jesus speaks of many who will come in Jesus' name claiming to be the Christ (Mt 24:5). Such persons are antichrists.

The apostle John, in his epistles, speaks of the antichrist (*antichristos*) four times (1 Jn 2:18,22; 4:3; 2 Jn 1:7). Often the term is used in a general or impersonal sense of one who opposes Christ. For example, anyone who denies that Jesus came in the flesh is an antichrist (2 Jn 1:7). Anyone who denies that Jesus is the Christ is the antichrist (1 Jn 2:22).

But perhaps there will be one personal antichrist in the future. Paul speaks of a "man of lawlessness" who will oppose God and set himself up in God's temple. But at the end, Jesus will destroy him by the splendor of his coming (2 Thess 2:3-8).

The purpose of the signs[2]

The signs remind us that there is evil in the world. There is both natural evil (famines and earthquakes) and moral evil (apostasy and tribulation). But the signs also remind us that God is in control of history and that he has a purpose for world history. The signs anticipate the return of Christ.

Even though the signs may suggest the return of Christ, in the end no one knows when Jesus will come again. "No one knows about that day or hour," Jesus said (Mt 24:36). The return of Christ will be unexpected. Jesus will come again like a thief in the night.

The signs call for watchfulness and readiness. Jesus said, "Keep watch because you do not know on what day your Lord will come" (Mt 24:42).

Study Questions

1.   Are the signs of Christ's return present or future? Explain.
2.   How is the delay of Christ's return grace for Jews and Gentiles?
3.   Who are the Antichrist and the antichrists?
4.   What is the purpose of the signs?
5.   **Essay:** Write an essay on whether we are in the end times or not.

---

[2]See A. Hoekema, *The Bible and the Future*, pp. 133-35.

CHAPTER 27

THE RETURN OF CHRIST

The end of world history for the Christian theologian is the return of Jesus Christ. The Old Testament expects the future day of the Lord (Yahweh); the New Testament eagerly expects the day of the Lord (Jesus Christ).

The New Testament tells us that when Christ comes there will be a resurrection and a final judgment.

The day of the Lord

The New Testament has frequent references to the day of the Lord, when Jesus will come again. There are a few basic terms that are used.

That time is called "the day of the Lord" (1 Thess 5:2; 2 Pet 3:10), "the day of Christ" (Phil 2:16), "the day of the Lord Jesus" (2 Cor 1:14), "the great day" (Jude 1:6), "the last day" (Jn 6:39,40,44,54) or simply "that day" (Mt 7:22; 2 Tim 1:12,18).

Sometimes that time is referred to as Christ's "coming" (*parousia*). Paul explains what will happen at "the coming of our Lord Jesus Christ" (1 Thess 2:1,8). The disciples looked for signs of Jesus' coming (Mt 24:3).

At times the return of Christ is called his "revelation" (*apokalupsis*). Paul waits for the revelation of Christ (1 Cor 1:7; 2 Thess 1:7). Peter tells us that our faith will be proved genuine at the revelation of Jesus Christ (1 Pet 1:7).

Sometimes the return is called the appearance (*epiphaneia*) of Christ. Paul talks of "the appearance of his coming" (2 Thess 2:8). He looks forward to the appearance of the glory of Jesus (Tit 2:13).

So what will the return of Christ be like?[1] First, it will be a personal and physical coming. The angels said, "This same Jesus . . . will come back in the same way you have seen him go into heaven" (Acts 1:11).

Second, it will be a visible coming. "All the nations of the earth . . . will see the Son of Man coming on the clouds of the sky" (Mt 24:30). John at Patmos was told, "Look, he is coming with the clouds, and every eye will see him" (Rev 1:7).

Third, it will be a sudden coming. The parable of the ten virgins illustrates the sudden and unexpected return of Christ (Mt 25:1-13).

Finally, it will be a glorious and triumphant coming. "The Lord himself will come down from heaven with a loud command, with the voice of the archangel and with the trumpet call of God" (1 Thess 4:16).

The resurrection of the dead[2]

The resurrection of the dead will occur when Jesus returns. This is a prerequisite for the final judgment.

Scripture speaks of the resurrection of the believers and unbelievers occurring together. The book of Daniel speaks of the resurrection of all persons, "some to everlasting life, others to shame and everlasting contempt" (Dan 12:2). Jesus also teaches such a general resurrection: "a time is coming when all who are in their graves will hear his voice and come out—those who have done good will rise to live, and those who have done evil will rise to be condemned" (Jn

---

[1]See L. Berkhof, *Systematic Theology*, pp. 704-6.
[2]See A. Hoekema, *The Bible and the Future*, pp. 239-52.

5:28-29). The book of Acts also refers to "a resurrection of both the righteous and the wicked" (Acts 24:15).

But the emphasis of the New Testament is on the resurrection of the believers, those who are in Christ. At the return of Christ, "the dead in Christ will rise first" (1 Thess 4:16). Jesus promised that he would raise the believers at the last day (Jn 6:39-40,44,54).

In 1 Corinthians 15 we have the fullest treatment of the resurrection of the believer. There Paul affirms the necessity of the resurrection of the dead. The believer's resurrection depends on the resurrection of Christ, who is "the firstfruits of those who have fallen asleep" (1 Cor 15:20). At the sound of the trumpet, "the dead will be raised imperishable, and we will be changed" (1 Cor 15:52).

The last judgment[3]

After the resurrection of the dead, there will be a final judgment. Scripture talks of a "day of judgment" (Mt 11:22; 2 Pet 3:7).

It will be a dramatic moment: "When the Son of Man comes in his glory, and all the angels with him, he will sit on his throne in heavenly glory. All the nations will be gathered before him, and he will separate the people one from another" (Mt 25:31-33).

John saw "a great white throne and him who was seated on it." He also saw "the dead, great and small, standing before the throne, and books were opened" (Rev 20:11-12).

So who is the judge? In a sense, God the Father is the judge. Paul speaks of "God's judgment seat" (Rom 14:10). But Jesus Christ is the sovereign God who judges on behalf of the Father. The Gospel of John says that "the Father judges no one but has entrusted all judgment to

---

[3]See A. Hoekema, *The Bible and the Future*, pp. 253-64.

the Son" (Jn 5:22). Jesus is reigning for the Father until he hands over the kingdom to God the Father (1 Cor 15:24-28).

What then is the basis of Christ's judgment? Good works are important. John writes that "the dead were judged according to what they had done" (Rev 20:12). Matthew's account of the last judgment also emphasizes good works (Mt 25:34-46).

But in the end we are justified by our faith in Jesus Christ. In the end, our good works are not sufficient for our justification.

Scripture is clear about the centrality of faith. John writes: "Whoever believes in the Son has eternal life, but whoever rejects the Son will not see life, for God's wrath remains on him" (Jn 3:36). Paul writes: "There is now no condemnation for those who are in Christ Jesus" (Rom 8:1).

Of course, faith without works is dead. We will be judged on the basis of our faith that produces good works. If the good works are absent, where then is the faith?

Hell

Today there are many who deny the doctrine of hell. But this teaching is prominent especially in the teaching of Jesus, but also in the rest of Scripture.

The Greek word for hell is *gehenna*, and is used mostly by Jesus. One who is angry with his brother is "in danger of the fire of hell" (Mt 5:22). Those who commit adultery are in danger of hell (Mt 5:29-30). Even the Pharisees were in danger of hell (Mt 23:15,33).

Hell is a place of "eternal destruction" (2 Thess 1:9). There "the fire never goes out" (Mk 9:43). It is a place of "eternal fire" (Jude 1:7).

But those who have faith in Jesus will escape the punishment of hell.

The eternal kingdom of God

The original creation in all of its fullness was the kingdom of God. But sin ruined this kingdom. Yet the Old Testament expressed the hope of a new creation or kingdom.

The prophet Isaiah expressed the hope of the new kingdom of God: "The wolf will live with the lamb, the leopard will lie down with the goat . . . and the earth will be full of the knowledge of Yahweh" (Is 11:6-9).

Again, Isaiah said, "On this mountain Yahweh Almighty will prepare a feast of rich food for all peoples . . . he will swallow up death forever" (Is 25:6-8). The end of Isaiah prophesies "new heavens and a new earth" (Is 65:17).

The prophet Micah foretold the time when "every person will sit under his own vine and under his own fig tree, and no one will make them afraid" (Mic 4:4).

The prophet Ezekiel looked forward to a new covenant when God would dwell among his people: "My dwelling place will be with them; I will be their God, and they will be my people" (Ezek 37:27-28).

These are eschatological prophecies of the eternal kingdom of God. When Jesus came, the kingdom of God was partially fulfilled. But the complete fulfillment lies in the future.

The apostle John saw a vision of this eternal kingdom of God: "Then I saw a new heaven and a new earth" (Rev 21:1). John's vision then becomes picturesque: he saw a city like a cube, 2000 kilometers high and 2000 kilometers square. The streets of the city were made of gold, and the 12 gates were pearls. He saw a river with fruit-bearing trees along its banks. But there was no temple, because God and the Lamb are its temple (Rev 21 and 22).

A few things are evident from these pictures. First, heaven will not be "other-worldly." The Old and New Testaments use physical language to describe the future kingdom. The future kingdom is not just a new heaven but also a new earth. As always, biblical theology is wholistic.

This is confirmed by the doctrine of the resurrection of the body. Heaven will not be disembodied spiritual existence. Heaven will have a physical side to it.

Second, there will be perfect fellowship with God. John defines eternal life as knowing (or loving) God and Jesus Christ (Jn 17:3). The essence of the old and new covenants is fellowship between God and the believer. This fellowship will be perfected in the future.

Finally, there will be a situation of complete *shalom* or peace among the people and even the animals in heaven. Isaiah's prophecy of *shalom* will be fulfilled: there will be no more warfare; instead wild animals will live at peace with each other and with us humans.

This is the eschatological kingdom that we may look forward to.

Study Questions

1.   Give three terms for the return of Christ.
2.   Describe the future return of Christ.
3.   Why is the resurrection of the dead important?
4.   Will we be judged on the basis of our good works? Explain.
5.   **Essay:** Write an essay on John's view of heaven in Revelation 21 to 22.

APPENDIX A

A BRIEF HISTORY OF CHRISTIAN DOCTRINE

Theology is done in context. This brief history of doctrine may help the reader understand the historical context in which some of our Christian doctrines were developed.

The Early Church (33 - 500)[1]

The Christian church was born at Pentecost. The first Christian theologians after Jesus were the apostles and the other writers of the New Testament.

By the end of the first century (AD 99), we assume that all the apostles were dead. The next generation of Christian theologians is called the Apostolic Fathers, among whom are Clement of Rome, Polycarp and Ignatius. Their theology tends to be simple, but having a profound love for Jesus.

Ignatius, bishop of Antioch, is an example. He was arrested by Roman soldiers around AD 110 and taken to Rome to be martyred. On the way he wrote letters to six churches and to Bishop Polycarp, expressing his deep love for Jesus. Twice in his letter to the Romans, he even calls Jesus God. But he does not explain how the Father and Jesus can both be God while there is only one God.

---

[1]For the early church, see H. Boer, *A Short History of the Early Church* (Ibadan: Daystar, 1976).

The Christian church began in the Greek (eastern) part of the Roman Empire. An important question then was the relation between Christ and culture. Some early theologians rejected the Greco-Roman culture; others tried to contextualize the Gospel into their culture.[2]

Justin Martyr, who was martyred in Rome around 165, is an example of a contextualized Christian theologian. He argued for a "common ground between the Christian and the [Greek] philosopher."[3] In particular, he found the Greek philosophical concept of the Logos (Word) relevant. For him Jesus is the pre-existent Word who is the source of all truth. Justin Martyr is an example of responsible contextualization.

But there was also irresponsible contextualization, which we call syncretism. (Syncretism is the mixing of incompatible religious ideas.) In the 2nd century, Gnosticism was popular. Gnosticism thought that matter is evil and spirit is good. Gnostic sects claimed to have a secret path to escape the world of matter. The Creator God, they said, was bad. So Gnosticism rejected the Old Testament and its God. The Gnostics also created their own "Gospels," like the Gospels of Thomas, Philip and Mary, to take the place of our canonical Gospels.

Bishop Irenaeus, who was bishop in Lyon from about 178 to 200, was disturbed. Is Gnosticism true? What is true? Bishop Irenaeus concluded: if a teaching is apostolic, it is true; if it is not apostolic, it is not true. (The apostles, after all, were closest to Jesus.) The standards of orthodoxy are then the apostolic creed, the apostolic writings and the apostolic bishop. Since Gnosticism was not truly apostolic, it should be rejected. The Old Testament, which Jesus and the apostles assumed, was thus saved for the Christian church.

---

[2]See K. Bediako, *Theology and Identity* (Oxford: Regnum, 1992).
[3]K. Bediako, *Theology and Identity*, p. 143.

At the same time a wealthy businessman arrived in Rome. His name was Marcion. Marcion thought that the Old Testament God was radically different from the New Testament God. Marcion thus rejected the Old Testament and Jewish parts of the New Testament. But in 144 the church excommunicated him for his wrong ideas.

Meanwhile the Gospel was being contextualized into the Latin-speaking world. North Africa, and in particular Carthage (in present-day Tunisia), was a leader.

Tertullian (ca. 150-225) came from Carthage. On the one hand, Tertullian had a negative view of culture. In this sense, he opposed the contextualization of the Gospel into the Greco-Roman culture.[4] Yet Tertullian gave Latin form to theological concepts. God, he said, is one *substantia* (substance) and three *personae* (persons).

Cyprian (ca. 200-258) was a bishop of Carthage who was martyred in 258. He spoke of the unity of the visible church. He said, "There is no salvation outside of the church" (*extra ecclesiam nulla salus*). But which church is this? The Roman church or any visible church?

Meanwhile important things were happening in Greek-speaking Alexandria (in present-day Egypt). Clement of Alexandria (died ca. 215) tried to contextualize the Gospel into the Greek philosophical world. Again the Logos was an important Greek concept in this contextualization enterprise.[5]

Clement's brilliant student was Origen (ca. 182-251), who was also from Alexandria. Among other things, Origen said that the pre-existent Son is eternally begotten from the Father. In other words, since the Word is God's Son, he is begotten; but as God he is begotten eternally, not in time.

---

[4]See K. Bediako, *Theology and Identity*, pp. 100-126.
[5]See K. Bediako, *Theology and Identity*, pp. 174-207.

A presbyter from Alexandria disagreed. Arius (died 336) said that since God is one, the Son or Word cannot be God. There was a time, he said, when the Son or the Word did not exist. The Son, he thought, was not eternal.

But Athanasius (ca. 295-373) strongly objected. If the Son (the Word) is not God, how then can we be saved? Our salvation depends on the divinity of Christ, for only God can pay for the sins of the whole world.

So the Council of Nicea (325) said that the Son is *homo-ousios* (of the same essence) as the Father. Father and Son are equally God. The Council of Constantinople (381) said that the Holy Spirit is also divine.

But if Jesus is God, what is the relation between the divine nature and human nature of Christ? Nestorius (died after 439) is thought to have said that Jesus was two persons: a divine person and a human person. This view was rejected by the Council of Ephesus in 431. Jesus, this Council said, is only one person.

On the other hand, Cyril, bishop of Alexandria from 412 to 444, apparently said that Jesus had only one divine-human nature.

But the Council of Chalcedon (451) said that Jesus is one person with two natures—a divine nature and a human nature. Most of our churches today accept the Creed of Chalcedon.

But the Coptic Church in Egypt, for political and theological reasons, disagreed with Chalcedon. The Coptic Church was Monophysite, saying that Jesus had only one divine-human nature. But if Jesus has only one mixed nature, then God necessarily suffered on the cross.

The Nestorian churches also rejected Chalcedon, partly for political reasons. The Nestorian Christians planted many non-Western churches throughout Asia.

Meanwhile the Latin part of North Africa produced a great theologian. His name was Augustine (354-430). Augustine became bishop of Hippo in present-day Algeria. Augustine longed for a mystical union with God. At the beginning of his *Confessions*, he said, "Our heart is restless until it finds rest in Thee."

Augustine resisted God until his conversion in 386. After his conversion Augustine believed that it was only the grace of God that converted him. So Augustine developed the doctrine of election and irresistible grace. Ultimately, for him, it is God who converts a person.

But a British theologian called Pelagius (died ca. 420) disagreed. He thought that a person's human will is free to choose for or against God.

In 476 the Germanic tribes invaded Rome again and deposed the last Roman emperor in the West. The period of the early church in the West ended at the end of the 5th century. The Middle Ages had begun.

The Middle Ages (500 - 1500)[6]

The thousand years of the Middle Ages were different in the East and the West. Culture played a role: the Eastern Orthodox churches were Greek; the Western church was Latin.

Historical factors also played a role. Western Europe entered a period of cultural darkness with waves of foreign invasions; the Eastern or Byzantine Empire maintained much of its former glory. But Islam rose in 622 and posed a challenge especially to the East.

Three Eastern church councils were held at this time. The second Council of Constantinople (553) affirmed the unity of Christ's two natures. In so doing, they affirmed theopaschitism or the suffering of God.

---

[6]See D. Jowitt, *Christianity: A Concise History* (Ibadan: Kraft, 2010) for this period.

The third Council of Constantinople (680-681) taught that Jesus, who has two natures, also has two wills. The second Council of Nicea (787) allowed the use of icons or religious pictures in the churches.

In the West, the Catholic Church entered 500 years of darkness from 500 to 1000. Many people groups, including the Muslims, repeatedly invaded Europe in these years.

But by the year 1000 Europe emerged from this period of darkness. The High Middle Ages are from 1000 to 1350. Some great theologians arose in this period.

Anselm (1033-1109) was an Italian who became Archbishop of Canterbury. Anselm believed in the harmony of faith and reason. As a bird has two wings, so a theologian should use both faith and reason to understand God.

Anselm developed the satisfaction theory of the atonement. His book *Cur Deus Homo* (Why Did God Become Man?) argues that God the Son became man in order to satisfy the honor and justice of God.

Abelard (1079-1142) was a theologian in France. He rejected Anselm's satisfaction theory of the atonement and put forth the moral influence theory. He thought that Jesus came to the earth only to teach us about love.

Thomas Aquinas (1225-1274) was the greatest theologian of the Middle Ages. He too believed in the harmony of faith and reason in theology. Aquinas developed five rational proofs for the existence of God.

But the church in the Middle Ages became corrupt. Corruption, sexual immorality and power politics often characterized the life of the church. This raises the question: what is the church?

In England, John Wycliffe (ca. 1326-1384) said that the church of Christ is not the corrupt Catholic Church but rather the totality of the true believers. Wycliffe also wanted the people to go back to the

Scriptures. So he and his associates translated the Bible into the English language.

In Bohemia, which is in the present-day Czech Republic, John Hus (1373-1415) also criticized the corruption of the institutional church. For him too the church is only the true believers (the so-called invisible church). John Hus was burned at the stake for his criticism of the Catholic Church.

Reformation and Post-Reformation (1500–1700)

By 1500 the Roman Catholic Church was in need of reform. There was a serious problem with the Church's morals and its doctrines.

So Martin Luther (1483-1546) was used by God to reform the church. In 1517 Luther hammered the *95 Theses* to the church door in Wittenberg, protesting the Catholic system of indulgences.

The Catholic system of indulgences presupposed a theology of justification by faith and works. But after a careful study of Scripture, Luther became convinced that we are justified only by faith in Jesus Christ. This was a liberating discovery for him. We no longer have to earn our salvation by doing enough good works.

In Switzerland two Reformers continued Luther's reformation. Ulrich Zwingli (1484-1531) was the reformer in Zurich. John Calvin (1509-1564) was the reformer in Geneva. They are the founders of the Reformed or Calvinistic churches.

The Protestant church in England was called the Anglican Church. In 1563 this church adopted the *Thirty-Nine Articles of Religion* which has been a doctrinal standard of the Anglican Communion until this day.

Luther, Zwingli and Calvin taught and practiced infant baptism. But other Reformers disagreed with this practice. They were called

Anabaptists. They believed that faith is a precondition for baptism. The Anabaptist movement began in the 16th century; the Baptist movement began in the 17th century.

The 17th century was a period of Protestant orthodoxy. Coherent systematic theologies were developed in this period. Protestant Christianity was presented in a rational way.

But reason by itself is not enough. The great systematic truths of the Bible need to be applied in the Christian's life. Pietism was the movement that stressed the personal, experiential side of the Christian faith.

The Modern Period (1700 – Present)

The 18th century in Europe was the Age of Reason. In the Middle Ages, reason was an ally to faith and revelation; now reason questioned and challenged faith and revelation. Reason was now often put above revelation.

This was partly a result of the rise of science. Science and reason questioned many of the doctrines of Scripture.

In 1748, for example, David Hume published his *Essay on Miracles*, which claimed that miracles are unscientific and thus did not happen. Other rationalists denied the divine inspiration of Scripture, the divinity of Christ and other basic doctrines of the church.

Rationalism led to 19th century liberalism. Adolf von Harnack (1851-1930) was a leading German Liberal. He denied the divine authority of Scripture, the divinity of Christ and the substitutionary atonement of Jesus. These doctrines, he thought, were not scientific or rational. Instead, Harnack talked of the goodness of God and the goodness of humanity. Jesus was a good prophet, preaching the message of love.

Liberalism is a contextualization of the Gospel into the European culture. But in the end it is European syncretism. It is a mixture of the European scientific culture with the Gospel. For liberalism Jesus is the "Christ of culture."[7] Jesus was made to conform to the European culture. This is syncretism.

Evangelicalism reacted against rationalism and liberalism. Evangelicals called the church back to the fundamental teachings of the Bible.

John Wesley (1703-1791) was a leading Evangelical of this period. Wesley insisted on the authority of Scripture and the necessity of personal conversion and holiness. His brother Charles Wesley (1707-1788) expressed this theology in music. The Methodist church proceeded out of the work of the Wesleys.

The Evangelical movement flourished in the 19th and 20th centuries. The Evangelical faith is based on the conviction that the Bible is the Word of God. Evangelicals believe in the divinity of Christ and the substitutionary atonement of Jesus. They believe in the necessity of personal conversion and sanctification. The great age of missions in the 19th and 20th centuries was a direct result of Evangelicalism. Evangelicals were also leaders in the anti-slavery movement.

A particular form of Evangelicalism is Pentecostalism. The origins of Pentecostalism are usually traced back to the Asuza Street revival in Los Angeles in 1906. Classic Pentecostalism teaches that baptism in the Holy Spirit is a second blessing which is evidenced by the speaking in tongues.

In Europe the 20th century opened with the brutal First World War (1914-1918). Tens of millions of people were killed. It became evident that mankind is deeply sinful. The liberal view of the goodness of mankind was inadequate.

---

[7]See H. Richard Niebuhr, *Christ and Culture* (New York: Harper, 1951), pp. 91-101.

Neo-Orthodoxy arose after the First World War. Karl Barth (1886-1968) was the founder of this movement. Neo-Orthodoxy talked of the sinfulness of humanity and the justice and holiness of God. The Word of God judges our human culture.

Neo-Orthodoxy is christocentric. Jesus is the one who reveals God. Jesus for them is the final Word of God. The Word of God is also found in Scripture, but Neo-Orthodoxy denies that the Bible is the Word of God. Instead, they claim that it contains the Word of God and it can become the Word of God. (In this sense the label Neo-Orthodoxy is useful: the movement is more orthodox than liberalism but not fully orthodox in the traditional sense of the term.)

The second half of the 20th century saw the rise of liberation theology. Liberation theology is concerned with the liberation of people from socio-economic bondage.

(Liberation theology should not be confused with liberalism. Liberalism is a *free way* of thinking; liberation theology is concerned with socio-economic *freedom*.)

A founder of liberation theology is Gustavo Gutierrez, a theologian from Peru. In 1971 he published in Spanish his *A Theology of Liberation*. The work calls for the socio-economic liberation of the poor and oppressed in the world. But for Gutierrez salvation or liberation is mostly horizontal or social; he doesn't speak much of the vertical or spiritual salvation.

In 1970 the black American theologian James Cone published *A Black Theology of Liberation*. In this work, Cone called for the liberation of the blacks from the whites. He even called God and Jesus black.[8]

During our present age, feminists also demand liberation from alleged oppression by men. Other interest groups are also preaching liberation.

---

[8]J. Cone, *A Black Theology of Liberation*, 2nd ed. (Maryknoll: Orbis, 1986).

The 21st century has a wide spectrum of theologies, many of which began in the preceding century or centuries. Each theology tries to make the message of the Bible relevant to its time. A critical theologian should judge to what extent these theologies are faithful to Scripture.

African Christian Theologies

African Christian theology in the non-formal sense is as old as Christianity in Africa. Any time an African—whether literate or illiterate—prays or sings or preaches, there is non-formal African Christian theology.

However, African Christian theology in the formal sense began in the 20th century. African Christian theology places the Gospel into the African context.

But what is the African context? Each African ethnic group has its own context. So there are many African contexts. Also, we should distinguish between the traditional African context and the contemporary urban context.

We can probably speak of three or four African Christian theologies today that have developed in the African context (or contexts).

First is *inculturation theology*. Inculturation theology places the Gospel into the traditional African context. Inculturation theology in the formal sense began in Catholic Francophone Africa in the 1950s.

Bénézet Bujo writes: "the first African who can be called an African theologian was Vincent Mulago, a Catholic priest from the then Belgian Congo."[9] In 1956 he published a book on Bantu life unity. In the same year a group of African priests published a collection of essays in French entitled *Des Prêtres Noirs s'interrogent* (Black Priests Ask).

---

[9]B. Bujo, *African Theology in its Social Context* (Nairobi: Paulines Publications, 1992), p. 55.

The 1960s saw the formation of the All-Africa Conference of Churches (AACC). In 1969 the AACC meeting in Abidjan said: "African Theology is 'a theology based on the Biblical faith of Africans, and which speaks to the African soul.'"[10]

African Christian theology is contextualized theology. Sometimes it is clearly syncretistic. Bolaji Idowu, for example, praised the traditional (pagan) "faithful remnant whose loyalty to the religion of their forbears will continue steadfast."[11]

But other inculturation theologians are not syncretistic. Harry Sawyerr, for example, believes that since there is one eternal Word of God, there will be one Christian theology. African Christian theology will look for the "common ground [which] exists between Christianity and the African traditional religious thought-forms."[12]

Osadolor Imasogie also called for an inculturation of the Gospel. For him the African culture and worldview are sources of theology; but the primary sources of theology are the Holy Spirit and Scripture.[13] Imasogie's inculturation theology is contextualized but not syncretistic.

The second kind of African Christian theology is *African liberation theology*. Formal liberation theology in Africa began in South Africa in the 1970s as a Christian response to apartheid. This theology began as Black Theology. Allan Boesak and Desmond Tutu were leaders in this movement.

The context of liberation theology is not the traditional African context but rather the contemporary political and socio-economic

---

[10]Quoted by A. Shorter in *African Christian Theology—Adaptation or Incarnation?* (Maryknoll: Orbis, 1977), p. 23.

[11]B. Idowu, *African Traditional Religion: A Definition* (London: SCM, 1973), p. 208.

[12]H. Sawyerr, "What is African Theology?" in *A Reader in African Christian Theology* (London: SPCK, 1997), p. 17.

[13]O. Imasogie, *Guidelines for Christian Theology in Africa*, pp. 72-74.

context. Liberation theology is concerned with the contemporary realities of poverty and political oppression.

Bénézet Bujo, for example, is concerned with the mass poverty in Africa. He thinks that the theology of inculturation is irrelevant to the contemporary African. Yet he appeals to an idea of the ancestors in his struggle for socio-economic liberation.[14]

A third kind of African Christian theology is *African evangelicalism*. At first glance, African evangelicalism resembles missionary theology. But a closer look reveals significant differences.

The early missionary theology in Africa was often other-worldly and individualistic. But, according to one author, "the missionary legacy has vanished with scarcely a trace, for it is terrestrial rewards that feature so prominently in African Christianity now."[15]

This may be an overstatement; but the fact is that African evangelicalism believes that God will meet our personal needs. African evangelicalism believes in God's power to supply our physical needs.

African evangelicalism in its ideal form is wholistic. It is concerned with both our spiritual salvation and our present physical needs.

But a prominent distortion of this Gospel has arisen. It is called *prosperity theology*. In reaction to missionary other-worldly theology, prosperity theology is very much this-worldly.

This theology, which has American roots, began in Africa in the 1980s with preachers like Benson Idahosa and David Oyedepo. Their teaching is simple: God desires that every person be rich. If a Christian is faithful, he or she will be prosperous.

---

[14]B. Bujo, *African Theology in its Social Context*, pp. 66; 69-106.

[15]P. Gifford, *African Christianity: Its Public Role* (Bloomington: Indiana University Press, 1998), p. 340.

But Femi Adeleye calls this theology a strange Gospel and a counterfeit faith. For him prosperity theology is a gospel of greed. Adeleye says that prosperity theology is a distortion of the Gospel.[16]

Prosperity theology is a non-formal theology contextualized into the contemporary African context. But it is clearly syncretistic.

The Christian church throughout the last 2000 years has always done theology. Often this theology has been faithful to the Word of God. But there have also been significant distortions of the Gospel in the history of theology.

The center of gravity of the Christian church has now shifted from Europe and America to the global South, including Africa. It is now Africa's turn to take a lead in doing responsible contextual theology.

---

[16]See F. Adeleye, *Preachers of a Different Gospel* (Bukuru: Africa Christian Texbooks, 2011).

BIBLIOGRAPHY

Aben, Tersur. *African Christian Theology*. Bukuru: African Christian Textbooks, 2008.

Achtemeier, Elizabeth. *Nature, God, and Pulpit*. Grand Rapids: Eerdmans, 2008.

Adeleye, Femi. *Preachers of a Different Gospel*. Bukuru: African Christian Textbooks, 2011.

Appiah-Kubi, Kofi. "Christology". In Parrat, J. (ed.). *A Reader in African Christian*. London: SPCK, 1997, pp. 65-74.

Asamoah-Gyadu, J. Kwabena. *Contemporary Pentecostal Christianity*. Eugene: Wipf & Stock, 2013.

Augustine, Aurelius. *The Confessions of St. Augustine*. Translated by E.B. Pusey. London: Dent, 1907.

Aulen, Gustav. *Christus Victor*. Translated by A.G. Herbert. New York: Macmillan, 1969.

Barth, Karl. *Church Dogmatics*. 14 volumes. Translated by G. Bromiley. Edinburgh: T&T Clark, 1936-1975.

Bediako, Kwame. *Theology and Identity*. Oxford: Regnum Books, 1992.

Berkhof, Hendrikus. *Christian Faith*. Revised edition. Translated by S. Woudstra. Grand Rapids: Eerdmans, 1986.

Berkhof, Louis. *Systematic Theology*. Edinburgh: Banner of Truth, 1939.

Bird, Michael. *Evangelical Theology*. Grand Rapids: Zondervan, 2013.

Boesak, Allan. *Farewell to Innocence*. Maryknoll: Orbis, 1976.

Boer, Harry. *A Short History of the Early Church*. Ibadan: Daystar, 1976.

Boff, Leonardo. *Holy Trinity, Perfect Community*. Translated by P. Berryman. Maryknoll: Orbis, 2000.

Boice, James. *Foundations of the Christian Faith*. Downers Grove: InterVarsity Press, 1986.

Bray, Gerald. *God is Love: A Biblical and Systematic Theology*. Wheaton: Crossway, 2012.

Bujo, Bénézet. *African Theology in its Social Context*. Translated by J. O'Donohue. Nairobil: Paulines Publications, 1992.

Bultmann, Rudolf. *Kerygma and Myth*. Translated by R. Fuller. New York: Harper, 1961.

Calvin, John. *Institutes of the Christian Religion*. Translated by F. L. Battles. Philadelphia: Westminster, 1960.

Cone, James. *A Black Theology of Liberation: 2ⁿᵈ edition*. Maryknoll: Orbis, 1970, 1986.

Dunning, H. Ray. *Grace, Faith and Holiness: A Wesleyan Systematic Theology*. Kansas City: Beacon Hill Press, 1988.

Erickson, Millard. *Christian Theology*. Grand Rapids: Baker, 1983.

Fackre, Gabriel. *The Christian Story: 3ʳᵈ edition*. Grand Rapids: Eerdmans, 1996.

Frame, John. *No Other God: A Response to Open Theism*. Philipsburg: P&R, 2001.

Galadima, Bulus. *A Study in Non-Formal African Theology*. Ph.D. thesis. Deerfield: IL: Trinity International University, 1995.

Gifford, Paul. *African Christianity: Its Public Role*. Bloomington: Indiana University Press, 1998.

Green, Michael. *I Believe in the Holy Spirit*. Revised edition. . London: Hodder and Stoughton, 1985.

Grudem, Wayne. *Systematic Theology*. Leicester: InterVarsity, 1994.

Gutierrez, Gustavo. *A Theology of Liberation*. Translated by C. Inda and J. Eagleson. Maryknoll: Orbis, 1973.

Hoekema, Anthony. *Created in God's Image*. Grand Rapids: Eerdmans, 1986.

Hoekema, Anthony. *Saved by Grace*. Grand Rapids: Eerdmans, 1989.

Hoekema, Anthony. *The Bible and the Future*. Grand Rapids: Eerdmans, 1979.

Idowu, Bolaji. *African Traditional Religion: A Definition*. London: SCM Press, 1973.

Imasogie, Osadolor. *Guidelines for Christian Theology in Africa*. Achimota: Africa Christian Press, 1983.

Jacob, Edmund. *Theology of the Old Testament*. Translated by A. Heathcote and P. Allcock. New York: Harper, 1958.

Jastrow, Robert. *God and the Astronomers*. New York: Norton, 1978.

Jones, Kenneth E. *Theology of Holiness and Love*. Prestonburg: Reformation Publishers, 1989.

Jowitt, David. *Christianity: A Concise History*. Ibadan: Kraft Books, 2010.

Kabasélé, François. "Christ as Chief". In Schreiter, R. (ed.). *Faces of Jesus in Africa*. Maryknoll: Orbis, 1991, pp. 103-15.

Kato, Byang. *Biblical Christianity in Africa*. Achimota: Africa Christian Press, 1985.

Kato, Byang. *Theological Pitfalls in Africa*. Nairobi: Evangel, 1975.

Kolié, Cécé. "Jesus as Healer?". In Schreiter, R. (ed.). *Faces of Jesus in Africa*. Maryknoll: Orbis, 1991, pp. 128-50.

Kunhiyop, Samuel. *African Christian Theology*. Bukuru: Africa Christian Textbooks, 2012.

Ladd, George E. *A Theology of the New Testament*. Grand Rapids: Eerdmans, 1974.

Luther, Martin. *Luther's Works*. 55 volumes. Edited by J. Pelikan and H. Lehman. Philadelphia: Muhlenberg Press/ Fortress Press, 1957-1986.

McCain, Danny. *We Believe*. 2 volumes. Bukuru: Africa Christian Textbooks, 2004, 2006.

McGrath, Alister. *Christian Theology: An Introduction*. Second edition. Oxford: Blackwell, 1997.

Mbiti, John. *African Religions and Philosophy*. New York: Doubleday, 1970.

Michael, Matthew. *African Christian Theology and African Traditions*. Kaduna: Yuti, 2011.

Milne, Bruce. *Know the Truth*. Leicester: Inter-Varsity, 1982.

Minear, Paul. *Images of the Church in the New Testament*. Philadelphia: Westminster, 1960.

Moltmann, Jürgen. *The Crucified God*. Translated by R. Wilson and J. Bowden. London: SCM Press, 1974.

Murray, John. *Redemption—Accomplished and Applied*. Grand Rapids: Eerdmans, 1955.

Mushete, Ngindu. "Unity of Faith and Pluralism in Theology". In Torres, S. and Fabella, V. (ed.). *The Emergent Gospel*. Maryknoll: Orbis, 1978, pp. 50-55.

Niebuhr, H. Richard. *Christ and Culture*. New York: Harper, 1951.

Nyamiti, Charles. *Christ as our Ancestor*. Gweru: Mambo Press, 1984.

Palmer, Timothy. *A Theology of the Old Testament*. Bukuru: Africa Christian Textbooks, 2011.

Palmer, Timothy. *A Theology of the New Testament*. Bukuru: Africa Christian Textbooks, 2012.

Palmer, Timothy. *Biblical Exegesis Handbook*. Bukuru: Africa Christian Textbooks, 2013.

Palmer, Timothy. "Jesus Christ: Our Ancestor?". *TCNN Research Bulletin 42*. Sept. 2013, pp.4-17.

Palmer, Timothy. *The Reformed and Presbyterian Faith: A View from Nigeria*. Bukuru: Africa Christian Textbooks, 2013.

Plantinga, Cornelius. *Not the Way It's Supposed To Be: A Breviary of Sin*. Grand Rapids: Eerdmans, 1995.

Pobee, John. *Toward an African Theology*. Nashville: Abingdon, 1979.

Ridderbos, Herman. *Paul: An Outline of his Theology*. Translated by J. De Witt. Grand Rapids: Eerdmans, 1975.

Ryle, J.C. *Holiness*. Ibadan: Amazing Grace Publications, 1994.

Sawyerr, Harry. *Creative Evangelism*. London: Lutterworth Press, 1968.

Sawyerr, Harry. *God: Ancestor or Creator?*. London: Longman, 1970.

Sawyerr, Harry. "What is African Theology?". In Parratt, J. (ed.). *A Reader in African Christian Theology*. London: SPCK, 1997, pp. 9-22.

Shorter, Aylward. *African Christian Theology—Adaptation or Incarnation?*. Maryknoll: Orbis, 1977.

Smedes, Lewis. *All Things Made New*. Grand Rapids: Eerdmans, 1970.

Spykman, Gordon. *Reformational Theology*. Grand Rapids: Eerdmans, 1992.

Stinton, Diane. *Jesus of Africa*. Nairobi: Paulines Publications, 2004.

Stott, John. *The Cross of Christ*. Downers Grove: InterVarsity Press, 1986.

The Book of Common Prayer. Abuja: The Church of Nigeria (Anglican Communion), 2007.

Pinnock, C. (ed.). *The Openness of God*. Downers Grove: InterVarsity Press, 1994.

Tiessen, Terrance. *Providence and Prayer*. Downers Grove: InterVarsity, 2000.

Waruta, D. "Who is Jesus Christ for Africans Today? Prophet, Priest, Potentate". In Schreiter, R. (ed.). *Faces of Jesus in Africa*. Maryknoll: Orbis, 1991, pp. 52-64.

Wesley, John. *The Works of John Wesley*. 14 volumes. Edited by T. Jackson. Peabody: Hendriksen, 1984.

Wiesel, Elie. *Night*. Translated by Stella Rodway. New York: Avon Books, 1960.

Williams, J.R. *Renewal Theology*. Grand Rapids: Eerdmans, 1996.

Wolff, H.H. *Anthropology of the Old Testament.* Translated by M. Kohl. London: SCM Press, 1974.

Wolterstorff, Nicholas. *Until Justice and Peace Embrace.* Grand Rapids: Eerdmans, 1983.

www.ingramcontent.com/pod-product-compliance
Lightning Source LLC
Chambersburg PA
CBHW060751050426

42449CB00008B/1364